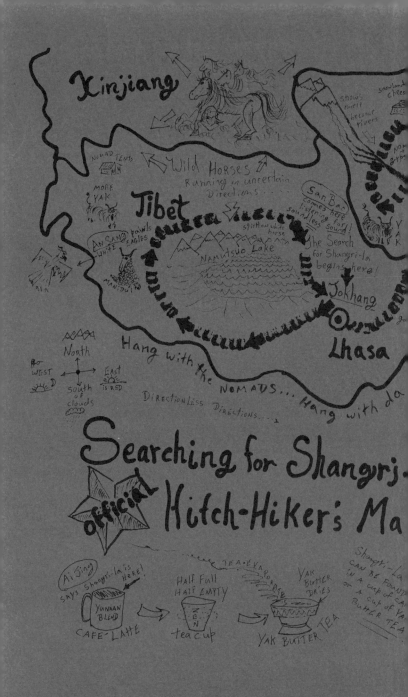

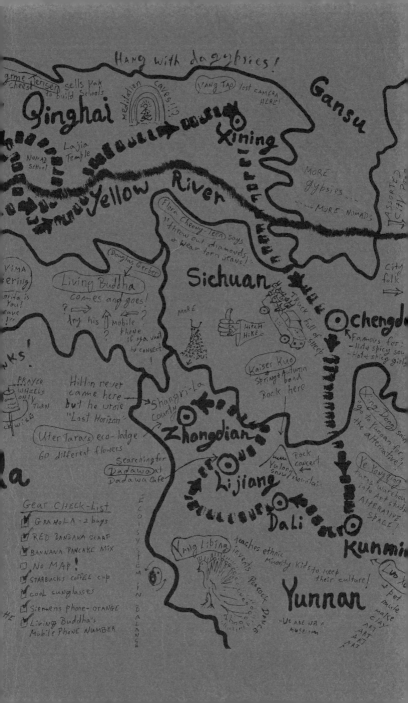

Searching for
# Shangri-la
ষ্ম་শ্রিষ্ট্রিষ্ট্রিষ্ট্রিষ

An Alternative Philosophy Travelogue

Laurence J. Brahm

高等教育出版社
HIGHER EDUCATION PRESS

Some Tibetans believe our present world of war, disease, corrupt inequality and environmental desecration, is the self-destructive age of Kali, to be followed by

a new age of peace, ethnic harmony, environmental balance, and human dignity, yet to come. This future is Shambhala, sometimes called Shangri-la.

# Questions No Answers

Everyone asked me why I came to China. They used to ask me why I came to China, as if there was some fault, some strange reason. They keep asking me this question, even today. The truth is I do not have an answer. So I used to make up answers.

As a student, I worked as a tour guide taking American tourists around China. They always asked me why I came to China. I told them I did not have an answer. So they gave me an answer. They would whisper among themselves that I must have been the child of missionaries. I said no. They did not believe me. So after a while, I just told everyone that I was a child of missionaries.

Then I became a lawyer, a business advisor, a writer, a consultant, a commentator, and then everyone wanted my comments on anything related to China. So I would comment. After all the comments, press interviews, board meetings, meetings with all those CEOs visiting China every year, the question would always come up again, why did I come to China.

Again, I had no answer. But there must be an answer they insisted. There must be an answer. Everything must have an answer, otherwise the market economy will collapse as we cannot sell books which provide instant answers, products which are the answer to all questions, religious books and videos, and multi-media packaging of the answer which you need but just have to pay for, credit card will do and you can pay over Internet because it makes things so convenient. Do not tell me there is no answer, the answer must be

1

black and white, very clear, easily explained and capable of being packaged, franchised and distributed to all answer seekers seeking answers to the same question.

So I made up an answer. I told them that I came to China in 1981 inspired by Edgar Snow and Han Suyin, looking for Mao's China, and then I found Deng's China, and everyone was making too much money to talk about Mao anymore, so I stayed. This answer was always acceptable, because in the minds of those hearing it, I must be staying in China to make money. This sounded acceptable and constituted an answer. The truth is I did not have an answer.

I still do not have an answer. But now I am tired of China as I have

come to know it, making money, thinking about money, talking about money and living for money in its pure cash accountable form. It seems like they all worship money now. It seems like people are willing to sell anything in China for money and then sell what they buy to buy more money. This is not the China I came to 22 years ago. This was not why I came to China.

And now Beijing is no longer Beijing. The tree lined streets no longer have trees, only cement. The old courtyard houses are gone, replaced by cement. There seems to be nothing anymore here but traffic and cement. The city government seemed very proud of all of its cement because it looks just like the cement in America. So they are putting more cement on top of the cement, to try and look more like America.

And everybody calls me to ask for advice about how to make money in China. I guess the western businessmen have discovered that they can sell cement to China. So the phone is always ringing, ringing, ringing, ringing, ringing, ringing, and still ringing. Sometimes all of these businessmen calling me are upset that I have not read my e-mails. They expect me to wait for an e-mail, as if life was embodied in an electronic device. I would rather wait for nothing at all. I tell them to stop sending me e-mails because I won't sit in front of a computer screen waiting for their e-mails, waiting to die hoping to receive and send an e-mail. I cannot believe that life can be concentrated and reduced to one single digitized electronic message which is not even spelled correctly.

So they call me instead...and the ring, ring, ring, ring, ring, ring, ring, of a mobile phone goes ringing through the pulse of mind, for as long as you can stand the stress factor induced by excessive talking. To solve the problem, I gave everybody my mobile phone number, then switched off the phone, and bought another phone. This however, did not solve the problem.

So I began to ask myself the question, what am I doing here. Why did I come to China?

Then I had a dream. It came back to me every night. I had dreams of wild Tibetan ponies, white ponies running in uncertain directions. They were running across a vast Tibetan plain. It was surrounded by snow capped mountains, but they could not reach the mountains. I was not certain what direction they were running in, but I knew it was uncertain.

So I decided to follow the Tibetan ponies.

# Uncertain Directions

Where is Shangri-la? Is it Tibet? Some say Qinghai has more of that Tibetan feeling than Tibet, as if foreigners can determine better than Tibetans what Tibet should feel like. Some call this packaging.

The town of Lijiang, once an ancient kingdom in Yunnan, discovered a stone tablet with the Chinese characters Xiang-ge-li-la "Shangri-la" carved on the stone. So Lijiang advertised that it was Shangri-la. Tourists poured in. But another county called Zhongdian said that they were Shangri-la. Tourists started going there too. Then some people in Sichuan said that Shangri-la must be there too. They joined the dispute.

In fact, none of the officials in any of the self-proclaimed Shangri-la were looking for Shangri-la. Maybe they were just looking for tourist dollars on the back of packaging, franchising and distributing Shangri-la.

One day I sat in a Beijing Starbucks drinking coffee with pop singer Ai Jing. "A coffee shop is like a 'peach garden beyond the realm'," she explained. "If you want to find a place more open and expansive, well everyone has this in their mind, a place where they can feel freedom from urban hassles." I began to think about this, staring into a cup of café latte, looking for a connection to this peach garden thing.

I told her about the Tibetan ponies and my decision to follow them

SEARCHING FOR SHANGRI-LA

even if the direction was uncertain. I described the place where I kept seeing the ponies, a vast Tibetan plain surrounded by snow capped mountains. She said it sounded like Shangri-la, a place she had heard about, once, maybe twice. It could be found in a cup of café latte if one looked carefully enough. I looked into my cup of café latte and did not understand. She said I was not looking carefully enough.

The question is how to find a new direction without breaking course with the direction which you've been going for such a long time, because if you go in one direction long enough, it is easy to believe that this is the only direction, or the right direction, until you eventually run out of time. The only way to find a different course is to break the direction you have been going in. This may be done through definitive action, or inaction. To do this, you must stop everything you are doing and place it all in front of you like a deck of cards. Just spread it out in front of you. And then wait for the wind to blow away the cards.

I told Ai Jing that I was going out west, in search of an uncertain direction, in search of Shangri-la. "You ought to try," she said. "People talk of Shangri-la, but there are many controversies over where it really is. If you want to search for it, I think it must be in the west. Take a road and follow it, just go without any direction." She said if I was going to do this I should hitchhike. This was the best way to travel in China, because the direction would be uncertain and I would end up wherever I was dropped off. In such a case, when dropped off, I should keep walking, by myself, in a certain direction. If uncertain, I could always ask for directions.

So, I began walking. The direction was uncertain. So I began asking for directions.

Ai Jing says Shangri-la is HERE!

YUNNAN BLEND

CAFE-LATTE

# Conversation with a Yak Skull

I have watched you decompose.
I have seen eagles
pick at your sightless eyes
and ants
suck marrow from your bones.

I have wandered
to lost aeries
where eagles die.
Only to find
a talon
and a few feathers
rotting in the sun.

And there
in eve-tide stillness
I watched my shadow linger,
stretch
and dissolve into the night.
Where motionless
upon a distant land
time ceased to be measured
and all but the sky
was soon forgotten.

# TIBET

# Asking for Directions

Tibet. I left the airport. I began down the road toward Lhasa. I thought the search for Shangri-la should begin in Lhasa, but was not completely sure. So I started asking for directions.

It is said, upon arriving in Tibet, one should stop at a temple before entering Lhasa. But it is not said which temple to stop in or where one can find the particular temple. It is only said to be alongside the road. So I followed the road. Then I came to a temple. I did not know whether it was the right temple or not but went in anyways after asking the monks whether this was a temple. They said that there were a lot of temples on the road to Lhasa. They asked me which one I was looking for.

I asked a monk for directions. He offered me yak butter tea and I stopped looking for directions and drank the tea. It smelled of yak butter. The feeling was warm in the early Tibetan morning when sky is still cool and one feels that earth has not yet entirely awoken. The monk explained to me that if you want to begin searching for directions, you should begin with a cup of yak butter tea.

I tried to explain that I was searching for a place called Shangri-la but was not sure which direction to go in. Should I continue traveling to Lhasa or should I go somewhere else? The monks sitting

10

around were just hanging. They looked at me as if they understood an uncertainty in such a question which should not be answered with too much haste. They poured another cup of yak butter tea. I drank it.

Entering the inner chamber I found myself staring at the penetrating composure of Tara, the Tibetan goddess of mercy and knowledge, with eyes on her hands, feet, and forehead. She is said to see all, to know all. I stared at all of her eyes. She stared back with composure and sympathy. The room was consumed by silence of burning incense, scent decomposing in flame. The silence of incense was dissipated by the ring of a temple bell, sound of which was dissipated by the ring of my mobile phone. An old friend was calling. It was Douglas Gerber calling from Hong Kong. A high-flying corporate executive with an American multinational corporation, Douglas was quietly a practitioner of Tibetan Buddhist meditation. He told me that his teacher, the living Buddha Vera Ghyentse Rimpoche would be returning to Lhasa any day. He would probably be in Lhasa when I was.

Great! I would meet Rimpoche again after so many years. I asked Douglas when Rimpoche would arrive, where he would stay and when I could see him. I asked these questions with exactness. But Douglas did not know when Rimpoche would arrive or depart. Such details were unimportant. If I wished to see Rimpoche, I should look for him. Douglas gave me a couple of mobile telephone numbers of people who might know where Rimpoche would be, maybe not. Try calling the numbers, Douglas suggested. If I could not find the

11

living Buddha, I should not worry at all. The Buddha would find me.

I left the temple and hitchhiked down the road. The road passed a rock. There was a large Buddha carved on the rock, painted bright yellow and blue with a touch of green and red. White *hada* scarves and colored *jingfan* prayer flags blew in the wind where they had been placed.

You could see the statue from the road, but could not touch it unless you crossed the river. A young boy offered to lead me across the river. Placing his forehead against the hand of the statue he suggested that I do the same, ask for blessing and make a wish. I did the same and made a wish. I asked the stone Buddha to help me find Shangri-la. The young boy asked for money.

 # A Cup of Yak Butter Tea

For Tibetans, the greatest pilgrimage is to Jokhang Temple (Da Zhao Si in Chinese), the origin of Tibetan Buddhist philosophy. The process of arrival at Jokhang is a journey. Tibetans prostrate themselves each step of the way. Hands clasped in prayer are placed on forehead, chest, and waist, falling on both hands and knees, face down upon earth, stretched fingertips reaching forward. This is an act of ultimate submission to Buddha, Teachers, Bodhisattvas, and Guardians in this order. Each prostration brings them only one step further to where their fingertips stopped, only to begin prostrating again. This is how the pilgrimage to Jokhang temple begins and ends.

To prostrate repeatedly across the distance traveled on the journey to Jokhang Temple, is an act of faith Tibetans live for, a journey to be completed at least once in a lifetime. For some, this may require months of walking and prostrating, for others, years. On the plaza before Jokhang Temple, along the concentric roads winding around Jokhang Temple, one can see many Tibetans prostrating. Some have traveled long distances, others, entire lifetimes.

So for me, the search for Shangri-la began at Jokhang Temple. This was the logical place to begin such a search. Here, more than

14

1300 years ago during the Tang Dynasty's height, emperor Tang Taizhong presented princess Wen Cheng of his court to the Tibetan king Songtsen Gampo, an act of unity between two peoples. She brought with her an image of Sakamuni, the first Buddha. The temple was built around the image.

Around the temple concentric rings of roads unwind, lined with enormous brass Tibetan prayer wheels. There are written prayers tucked inside the wheels. If you turn them it is the same as saying the prayer. In this manner the temple is always surrounded by the whirling energy emitted from the concentric turning of wheels. Pilgrims coming to the temple must follow the cyclic path and turn wheels, all of them. You can turn them clockwise but not counter-clock-wise. Clocks cannot be turned backwards.

It is said that Princess Wen Cheng brought Buddhism to Tibet, and that she smiled like a Guanyin Bodhisattva, but remembered not to laugh. Jokhang became a center of learning, a center for the spread of Buddhist philosophy. From here the philosophy of ideal Shambhala, or "Shangri-la" extended to Nepal, Bhutan,

Prayer wheels turn clockwise
clocks cannot be turned backwards

Qinghai, Yunnan, and eventually throughout the world. So logically, the search for Shangri-la should begin at Jokhang Temple. I was to learn by coming to Jokhang Temple, that to begin such a search, one must begin by disengaging from the logical.

Such disengagement began when I entered the heavy red gate of Jokhang smothered in the smell of incense and yak butter oil. I entered the door and crawled up a narrow staircase to the rooftop looking for Nyima Tsering, one of 99 monks who administer Jokhang Temple. I found him in a room. He offered me yak butter tea. I began to look for Shangri-la in the cup of tea, and remembered to look carefully. I was not looking carefully enough.

Nyima Tsering complained about tourists. There were too many. While on one hand he was pleased that so many people wanted to come to Jokhang for knowledge of Tibetan Buddhist philosophy, he was disturbed by the number of cigarette butts and Kodak film cartons being left behind. Due to overwhelming international popularity of Tibetan philosophy and Shangri-la searching chic, the monks were now too busy sweeping up cigarette butts and used film cartons to have time for meditation, he complained. This was becoming a problem interfering with the process of concentration. How could monks teach Buddhist philosophy to visitors seeking

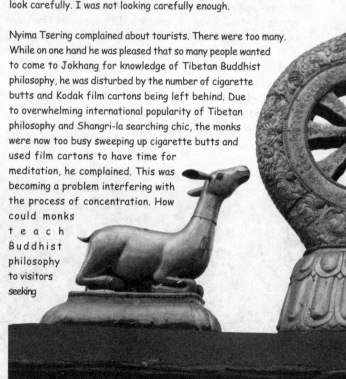

answers to questions, when the monks were so busy cleaning up the garbage visitors had left behind with their questions?

I stopped looking for Shangri-la to discuss this problem, hoping to provide an answer. Instead Nyima Tsering brought me onto the rooftop of Jokhang Temple to discuss Buddhist philosophy, while still complaining about extensive film box littering. I left the yak butter tea in his room, still hot. Eventually the tea would evaporate. Yak butter however, would remain.

"But now this is a problem," explained Nyima Tsering waving his hands excitedly from under saffron robes. "I feel both happy and sad. I am happy so many people want to understand our culture through Jokhang Temple. On the other hand, I worry that we have too many visitors. People come to Tibet with great hope of seeking Buddhist truths, however after arrival they cannot obtain what they want. As Buddhist monks we cannot introduce them properly to Buddhist Dharma, because there are many ideas which we monks including myself do not have time to understand. One thing we need is a quiet environment, a long time to meditate. This is prerequisite. But there is also a requirement in Buddhism that to save others' lives is to save all things with life. But before instructing others we should instruct ourselves. It is not enough to only have a splendid temple with lots of monks wearing these clothes inside," he pointed to his saffron robe. "The most important

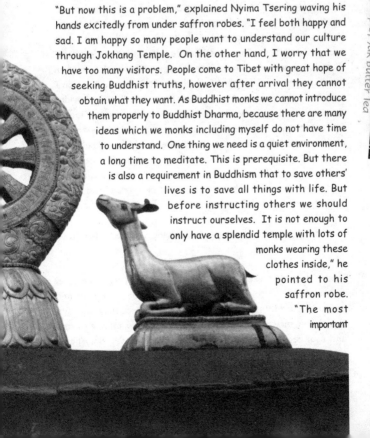

question is there should be masters and teachers inside too!" He was frustrated that "most of the monks are spending their time administering crowds visiting the temple, not meditating or cultivating the principles they should teach."

"But people are coming here because this temple is said to be the origin of Tibetan Buddhism," I asked. "So they're coming to the origin, right?"

"The origin of Buddhism is India," Nyima Tsering corrected me sharply. "However, it is a pity that Buddhism is now almost non-existent there because of past conditions, maybe destiny. Maybe it did not establish very solid roots there. Or maybe there were too many battles? Today we have to admit that the seeds of Shangri-la were only planted in the Qinghai-Tibetan plateau when Buddhism arrived. They sprouted, bloomed and fruited here. So I appreciate the vision of earlier generations, including Tibetan king Songsten Gampo. They changed Indian Buddhism into Tibetan Buddhism by combining its principles together with our environment, culture and customs. So we should feel thankful to our ancestors. But right now we have a new sense of urgency, as we their grandchildren inheriting it, should be responsible for protecting Shangri-la. This is a big urgent problem. If lost, it will not only be a loss for Tibetans, but a loss for the whole world."

"Are many people now coming to Jokhang Temple in search of Shangri-la?" I asked.

"Many, many, last week I received many from aboard. They said to me once they came to Lhasa, they felt complete calm and comfort, found things they had lost. However, once they return to their home, they become busy, time constraints pollute their heart and soul again. No matter how much more money they have, regardless of how big their factories, they cannot achieve real

18

human happiness. I think this is the power of Tibetan Buddhist philosophy. We may not have money, but we have the pride of knowing our heart is free and comfortable. In the era of my grandparents, life was poor, but relationships between people were much better. Really, there are two aspects to being happy, one is your material well being, the other is an open and free heart, without restrictions. Without this, the happiness of a human being is no different from an animal. If we only have material things, if you only have a beautiful home, big factory, then it is like raising pigs. Pigs are fed only to be killed."

I was perplexed by the analogy. "So when somebody comes to Jokhang Temple searching for Shangri-la, what do you tell them?

"If you want to look for Shangri-la, remember that the real freedom of a human being is found in the heart and soul. Racing in the process for economic development, we build factories, modernize technology. In the race for money, we lose our human nature, human morality, all polluted. Now the question is how to seek it back? This is not only a question of my people, but of people throughout the world right now. Many people have a good family, enough money to last several generations, but still do not feel happy. Why? Because it did not bring more happiness, rather it brought many frustrations. Therefore balance is missing. To have economy, industry and western modernization is not enough. If we lose the human side of our world, in the end, we will still have to find Shangri- la and bring it back."

"But is it really about to be lost?"

"If you ruin or pollute Shangri-la, no matter how much money you have, you can not buy the real thing back. It is a pity." Nyima Tsering shrugged under his robes. "People visiting Jokhang Temple are seeking inspiration, seeking Shangri-la. They should find more ways to purify themselves. You feel comfortable when you come to Jokhang Temple, but when you go back you have lost this feeling. It is only a temporary effect. The real effect depends on self understanding. Look for it in within, find the correct way to behave. I believe you do not need to come to Jokhang Temple, no need to come to Tibet. In your hometown, no matter whether this is in America, Europe, or any other country, you can find it. There is no restriction of nationality, border lines, time limit."

Nyima Tsering then began to connect life style with environment. "In Buddhism, all life is connected, including small life like ants. The best way of protecting the environment is through rebirth. For example, now I have an opportunity to become rich, to become a high ranking official, I can suddenly enjoy life, but I will refuse and say no, because I have a life to come back to. In order to become happy in the long run in my next life, I cannot accept this instant happiness blindly, which is not good for the future. As an example, a big weakness of our world is that people live for the short term. Only one life, so I have to grasp this opportunity; after I die I would not have any opportunity to enjoy life. So they ride roughshod to destroy this environment, to build so many factories to pollute it. This is criminal behavior. No matter how well developed your economy is, your environment can not compare with Shangri-la."

"The search for Shangri-la has brought me here, to Tibet." I asked, "Is this where I should come in search of Shangri-la?"

"I think Shangri-la is in Tibet," Niyma Tsering responded after a long pause. He seemed to be thinking about the question, pondering. "Why? Today we say the Qinghai-Tibetan Plateau is the last piece of clean land of humanity. Why? Because when my grandparents had the opportunity to ruin the environment, they said to themselves 'no, we will come back to this world, we will live in this

world again, our mother, so we should not hurt this mother.' So I feel Buddhism's concept of re-incarnation is associated with the environment, the importance of protecting even the smallest forms of life in our ecosystem. If we do not protect these cycles of life, then I think Shangri-la will disappear soon. In Buddhist teaching, there is no nationality. We are one family, our mother is the earth. Even little ants are our brothers and sisters. This makes the world interesting and meaningful. Although with all those many factories, airplanes which bring us convenience, you will find yourself even further away from real Shangri-la. You can not find Shangri-la on the airplane. You can only find it through your own self and behavior."

"So you're saying that destruction of our environment is now threatening Shangri-la?"

"Yes, natural resources must be used in a reasonable way," Niyma Tsering explained. "We want to survive, this is prerequisite. Tibetan Buddhism has a weak point in that it allows for the eating of meat, though this is forbidden in Buddhism. Why? Our Qinghai-Tibetan plateau is at a high altitude. Here it is cold, lack of oxygen, people are nomadic. Although killing life should be punished, human beings are more valuable. In order to survive on the Qinghai-Tibetan plateau, to kill some small life is permitted. But in the end, you should repay the killing. But multinational corporations now ride roughshod to expand damaging earth in the process. To satisfy their desire, they destroy mother earth in the name of competition. There will be a time, when the resources will be gone and what life can get from earth, will become less and less. Therefore Buddhism can see very far into the future. To survive in this world one should not seek too much luxury from life. Why? Life is re-incarnated. We must also consider the next generation, as they too must live on this earth. Despite all the scientific development and fancy technology, we can not move to live on the moon or sun.

If you pollute this earth, it will be very dangerous for the future of humanity. People should rationally calm down to think, to seek, to reconsider. Our ancestors may have been very poor, but I feel in some ways they were very rich. They had a better environment and more resources, so maybe they were richer than us. That is why I say we should look long term. Scientists use microscopes but can not see the future. Buddha has bright eyes and can see very far. He is responsible for all the life. We must be responsible for our own earth."

"So Shangri-la may be lost as we search for it," I thought out loud. According to Niyma Tsering, Shangri-la is not a place, but a cycle of our ecosystem, a state of mind. "So was I right to begin the search for Shangri-la by coming to Lhasa?" I asked him.

"In fact coming to Lhasa to take a look is correct. To come to feel is right. Human nature is to explore. But most important is to explore your own Shangri-la in your heart. This Shangri-La is forever, unlimited. But our universe earth mother is limited, so in our Buddhism, we say the real hero is not triumph over nature, is not triumph over our environment. The real hero is to triumph over our own frustration, the thing blinding your own search for Shangri-la. Selfish stupidity, unknown in Buddhism, is only of very short term benefit. In the end, there is nothing, except increased frustration and pressure for your psychology. I have money, I have factory, but I am not happy, even beggars are more relaxed than me. This is the search for Shangri-la."

I thought about what Niyma Tsering said, staring up at the pure blue sky stretching like endless sea above us to distant mountains behind Potala Palace. I was lost somewhere between blue and mountains when Niyma Tsering's voice cut clear between the blue.

"You can experience Shangri-la here. However the real Shangri-la

is not only found in Jokhang Temple. No matter where you go, there is no map of Shangri-la showing which route to take there. So I will tell you the way. Do not defeat outside enemies, instead defeat the enemy within yourself, selfishness. Eventually, Shangri-la can be found in your heart. It is not in Tibet, nor anywhere else. It is unfair to say this place is more Shangri-la than that place, because ultimately finding Shangri-la will depend on your own effort only. Shangri-la cannot be obtained by weapons, science or troops. The further you seek your Shangri-la, the further away you will be, you can search for it forever. We should use non-violence, kindness, wisdom and reason to look for our Shangri-la, which is also called spiritual civilization nowadays by us. You want to find the real Shangri-la? Look around you. I feel our world is a heaven. The hell in Buddhism is not created by God, but by yourself. Your own heaven or hell is all associated with your behavior. If human nature improves, the search for Shangri-la will become nearer."

Niyma Tsering then told me that the living Buddha of Jokhang Temple was locked in meditation, refusing to see anyone at all. But there might be a chance he would see me. Niyma Tsering led me across the rooftops of Jokhang, winding from one level to another, around a corner, twisting in one direction then another, across a small gallery, and into a tiny room. He indicated I should kneel on the ground, present the living Buddha with a white *hada* prayer scarf, and ask one question, maybe two.

The living Buddha of Jokhang Temple, a frail man with long thin white hairs on his eyebrows sitting cross legged. Smiling as I entered the tiny chamber he placed down long thin Buddhist texts he had been studying on a small table before him. Reaching over with both hands on each of my arms, he touched his forehead against mine. He knew I had come with many questions. Before I could ask, he listened.

"Today I am 85 years old and have researched many religions in my lifetime discovering that the greatest rationale can be found in Buddhism," explained the living Buddha in a soft voice as he sat alone on raised Tibetan bed with prayer scriptures laid before him, neatly yet somewhat scattered. "Through study I have discovered that to be pure is rational and very good. We must thank generations before for bringing Buddhism to Tibet which was their great contribution. One generation after another brought Buddhism here from India with great enlightened correct understanding and realization. This has served a great purpose. But in those days there was a discrepancy, being that Buddhism only circulated within the realm of Tibet and not beyond. But it is said that many Lamas are now disseminating Tibetan Buddhism throughout the world and this is of great purpose. I have heard that more and more people overseas are becoming interested in the notion of Shangri-la. This is the work and contribution of great teachers. But only after a Buddha becomes enlightened through correct study and bringing this enlightened way to others can one truly find the real Shangri-la."

"Is this why we have such a spread of Tibetan Buddhism overseas? It has almost become a fad." I was now on my second question.

"Overseas there are many Tibetan Buddhist missionaries, but not all are real. Some are fakes. Therefore one must be careful in searching for Shangri-la. It is not true that all Tibetan Buddhism is pure. Some things are being understood blindly without responsibility. It is best to go into the temple and study for twenty or thirty years and this will give great benefit. Only this way can enlightenment be released. This is the true premise for searching for Shangri-la. Otherwise you will blindly look for it but this is not necessarily a good thing. I hope you can find it. Approach this deeply, go further."

24

"Go further? How? What road to take?" Two and a half questions did not count three. Niyma Tsering blinked as the living Buddha spoke.

"You must find the correct road and this is most crucial. Buddhism has created many different schools. You must be careful. It is not that all of the schools are good. In the world there are many religions, but some are just blind. At the same time there are also many Buddhist schools of people following blindly, where incorrect explanations are given and people blindly follow others. Such schools are useless. Sakamuni's words are clear and rational. Believers cannot blindly believe words repeated at any time. What words are of use to you and what words are not? Those which are useless should be thrown away. Those which are worthwhile should be used. Do not believe blindly. Separate good from bad. This is a question of principle."

Leaving the meditation chamber of Jokhang Temple's living Buddha, I squinted in the sharp Tibetan sun. It cast shadows across the white rooftop of Jokhang Temple. The sun shifted position. The shadows grew into long thin lines, like a Dali painting. Stretching into infinity, they shifted. I watched the lines, the sun. I squinted. They shifted. Then I thought about searching for Shangri-la in a cup of tea. I went back to Niyma Tsering's chambers, looking for the cup I had been drinking that morning. Sure enough, I found the cup left behind. It was partly but not completely empty. It was full of yak butter but no tea. The tea had evaporated. The yak butter had already dried.

25

# Cold Thin Air

At 4:30 am Tibetan air is thin and cold. This makes climbing up a mountain in the dark difficult. Some people do not understand why one would want to climb a Tibetan mountain in the dark. It is like blindfolding oneself in a room and turning around in concentric circles until dizzy. Such behavior is not rationale or expected. It

exceeds realms of the precise. It lacks a particular answer.

I climbed the mountain. The silence of morning darkness was broken by the trickle of a running stream. I stopped for a drink and remembered to listen for a moment to the trickle. It was the sound of water becoming round for the first time upon touching the body of a rock. The water would never appear in this shape again after leaving the rock.

The patter of soft feet surrounded me. It was the sound of Tibetans traveling from distant places, to this place, to climb the mountain. They were young and old. An old woman was crippled. She supported herself on two sticks, her back bent over. She climbed the mountain like a deer. With a smile which lit the wrinkles of her cracked face, she offered to show me the way.

They came once a year. They climbed only in dark, before sunrise evaporated darkness. I followed them through dark. Following was the only way to find a way up the mountain, so I had to follow. There was no time to ask for directions. For them, this was pilgrimage and directions did not or should not be asked. So I followed them through a compact time span of thin Tibetan air. It tasted cold.

The Shoton Yogurt Festival occurs toward the summer's end, the best season for making yogurt, a critical sustenance for Tibetan people. It is a time of thanks before arrival of winter snows. It is a point in the transition of seasons when one may find a moment of introspection, a time to think about why one passes from one season to another with such ease, without paying attention to why.

The festival begins with pilgrimages to mountains beside temples which are built upon mountains. Inside these temples great Thanka are kept. Upon the Thanka canvasses are enormous paintings of the first Buddha, Sakamuni. The Thanka are so great in size that they may be spread across the surface of a mountain. Once a year, in the early morning over a hundred monks lost in trance of chants and drone of Tibetan horns will lift the great Thanka upon their shoulders to the height of a mountain, unrolling the Thanka within seconds before sunrise, so the first rays of light may touch the Buddha's face, so he may face the first rays of the sun, for just a second before they roll up the Thanka and put it away until the following year.

Colored papers representing elemental colors of life are shredded and tossed upon the Buddha's face together with offerings of white *hada* scarves and even money. Tibetan pilgrims crouch before the vast Thanka touching their heads to its image seeking blessing. Great chunks of turquoise embedded in brass or gold fittings braided into the hair of Kampa women touch the foot of Buddha. They press their heads to the vast Thanka in prayer. They press the foreheads of their children, of babies to the vast Thanka, seeking blessing. The yellow hat Lamas touch pilgrims with their yellow hats waiting with patience for blessing.

As the sun rises the mountain is no longer shrouded in darkness. The early sun rays touch Buddha's eyes, before which colored papers are tossed into a kaleidoscope of thin cold air which now becomes less thin, even warm.

A mountain covered with the face of Buddha, is overwhelmed by the prayer of Tibetan pilgrims, the sound of Tibetan long horns droning over chants of a hundred monks before golden temple rooftops, pagodas, touching air which is the space of eagles. Hallucinated by the smell of pine incense kindling in earthen burners, they dance in the wind. They do not know that prayer is given and blessing received, or that moments are a transition of seasons. They forget that air is thin, often cold.

# Soundless Sound

I met San Bao at Drepung Monastery, during unfolding of the great Thanka. In his own way searching for inspiration for new music. Recognized as China's greatest music composer today, from classic to pop, San Bao has created stars through his song writing and composition, writing hits for pop singers, movie directors like Zhang Yimou and Feng Xiaogang. I had seen him in concert in Beijing, conducting an orchestra playing his compositions, had listened to his music, felt his compassion. I did not expect however, that I would meet San Bao of all places, here in Tibet. Some might call this karma.

San Bao is actually ethnic Mongolian. The Mongolian people practice Tibetan Buddhism. Life style of mountains and grasslands are similar, nomadic spirit the same. One afternoon we sat together on the rooftop of Johkang Temple, drinking yak butter tea. The Potala Palace was within distance, the sky crystal blue, creating an illusion that one could reach out and touch the Potala. I tried to do this only to realize it was just an illusion, a distortion of perceptions. I began questioning my own perception of distance, space, time and music. We talked about sound.

"Your name 'San Bao' means 'three treasures', a concept in Tibetan Buddhism, right?"

"Really, this is my family name as I am the third brother, so the family called me San Bao 'third treasure'. My name San Bao is directly related to Buddhism. I do know, there is a San Bao Temple,

30

but the specifics of this place are not known to me. I do not disbelieve in re-incarnation. Everything does not have a conclusion. When one thing concludes a new one begins. A person's life forever is faced with making choices which require sacrifices. Gain from one's choice is also one's loss."

"Many people come to Tibet for inspiration," I wondered. "But why are we really here? What do you make of it?"

"Every person has a Shangri-la in their own mind," San Bao explained. "Every person is searching for this. But everybody has their own individual viewpoint, and each will use their own familiar way to find their own dream."

"So is this search for Shangri-la the driving force behind New Age music? Sounds of groups like Enigma?"

"From a music perspective, in the early 1980s so-called New Age or World Music emerged, reaching for ethnic elements at their root, fusing them into modern life style rhythm, creating pure sound. From this point onwards," San Bao explained, "a variety of diverse New Age Music forms sprang upon the scene. Many DJs and record engineers compiled raw and ethnic sounds, re-composing

them. Step by step a new epoch of music emerged. I feel that other cultural forms are also following this pattern, creating a kind of cross-over movement. Collectively the past twenty years may be viewed in retrospect as representing an epoch characterized by searching for the natural, for the pure. You see, music has many levels of comprehension. For instance, New Age Music has now become a fashion. Suddenly it appears that everyone is doing this, and it is now becoming overdone. Every person thinks as long as you get some primitive sounds, patch them together then you have the sound. For example, here in Lhasa I saw a Lama standing under a China Mobile advertisement, carrying a modern mobile phone. You will feel it is strange, a bit over-stated."

"Through New Age Music do you feel that composers and song writers are looking for something natural in ethnic sounds, which they feel is missing in modern urban life today?"

"Missing something?" San Bao asked himself out loud, looking up at pure blue sky above with waves of white clouds scattered in a distant illusion which gave a sense of proximity. "What are we all missing? Nobody can really answer this clearly. In reality, Shangri-la represents a state of composure. Regardless of where Shangri-la might be, this is really not so important. It is a life style, a state of composure, or the ideal in one's imagination." The clouds shifted, exposing more blue.

"Does this then represent an escape from modern urban yuppie utopia?" I asked.

"People living in cities for long periods can find themselves short of inspiration. But every person's inspiration is different. Sometimes I really want to go to some place which is far from the city, far from noise, maybe somewhere in the countryside, somewhere where there are no people, just close the door and stay alone by myself without anyone around. I am a person who has an extreme dislike of cities. I do not like any city at all. I do not know why. I have a feeling of special admiration for those artists, such as painters. If I was a painter I would certainly not live in the

32

city because such art can be completed by a single person alone. But for me, this is not the case. To be a music composer, I must work with song writers, musicians, recording engineers because my work requires many people to be involved collectively to complete. Qian Zhongshu once said, 'City people want to leave the city. Country people want to enter the city.' Regardless of career, marriage, people are just that way. I lived in this atmosphere and situation. So what I want is something different. In fact, however you look at it, it is just the same."

"The same, compared to what?" I was more confused. "Can you give me an example of what you mean?"

"Once I went to Yunnan," San Bao explained. "A friend there interviewed many people in rural villages, recording their life styles. He saw a local girl, who looked very open and expressive, so wanted to interview her. After talking for a while, he fixed a time for the interview. At the time he spoke, the girl was wearing traditional ethnic clothes, with a lot of character, very interesting. The next day when the village girl came for the interview, she did not wear her ethnic clothes but rather a modern dress with quite stylish shoes. Of course, this girl must have felt that she was dressed quite attractively. This shows a gap in culture. It is in fact very simple. It makes you really think to the point, what is beautiful?"

"So is this why you came to Tibet? What inspired you most on this trip?"

"Yesterday I drove to Namutsuo Lake. That is a beautiful lake. But the local nomads will probably ask you why bother driving a jeep for so long just to see a lake. We can see this lake every day and we do not see anything special there. The road to Namutsuo Lake was a feeling of traveling on a rough uncertain road. But then suddenly coming over the hill I saw the lake. It reminded me of once when I was driving a car in the U.S.A., suddenly I saw a city of neon lights appear in the desert, Las Vegas. I also had this same feeling. Of course both cases are two extremes of the same thing. But both situations created a feeling of shock after

33

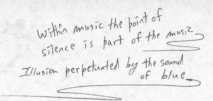

Within music the point of
silence is part of the music

Illusion perpetuated by the sound
of blue

apprehension."

"Experiencing shock after apprehension, maybe this is the search for Shangri-la. What do you think?"

"Many people search. This is just idealistic. The real dream is inside our own mind, if your heart can really find it. I like to go to really rural areas, where life is simple. In fact, it is not the place that I go to which is important, it is the process of getting there. People in the city however, often do not even have the time to consider this single question. Many workaholics probably do not even think that this is Shangri-la. But I am not a workaholic. So people often ask me as if I am strange, don't you feel bored going off to that kind of place? One person working for over a dozen hours at a time, isn't that boring? I say, yes, maybe it is boring for you, but every person is different and their feeling is different. Some people feel that if they have a nice house and steady job in the city, a nice family and good child, then that is enough. They feel that this is their Shangri-la, their dream. Is there anything wrong with that? In fact, they live a real life, and that is really great."

New World Music and new life style being fused with images and senses of the Qinghai-Tibetan plateau, a life style as far removed as one can get from that of urban yuppies seeking new world vision. The irony seemed striking. The question came back to what Niyma Tsering had said. Regardless of materialism, happiness was something you create with your own life style, your own means. Maybe this explains the rising international popularity of New Age Music. I asked San Bao, "Then isn't any kind of ethnic music entirely inter-related with life style?"

"Mongolian and Tibetan nomad music is completely integrated with the landscape," he explained pointing to a Mongolian yak hair standard propped on one rooftop of Jokhang. Integrated life style of both nomadic peoples had made this symbol of Mongolian power Tibetan as well. "In the vast grasslands, there are actually very few people. Their life style is to raise sheep and yak. Sometimes, there is only one person out there with the sheep and yak. Imagine,

34

alone all day on the grasslands with nobody to talk to. So the nomad will sing. But the space is too vast. Whoever person comes to such a place will feel expansive, as they cannot see anyone on the horizon. So what do you feel, what do you really want to do? Just scream out, because here you can let yourself go altogether. Here one's relationship with the forces of nature is the most basic. You can hear a person sing from a very great distance. Completely alone, one tends to sing to oneself, just to be happy. It is a pure relationship between an individual and their environment."

I noticed San Bao using a video camera to film two dogs sleeping in front of Jokhang Temple, the day before. I was really curious why he bothered to film a dog when so many other things were happening there. Before Jokhang Temple Tibetans from all parts of the plateau and monks from throughout the world, come to prostrate themselves before the temple doors. Hundreds of prayer wheels turn circulating a powerful energy. Pine incense burns giving the temple plaza a shrouded mysterious feeling. Visitors from every part of China and every country in the world come and go, purchasing Tibetan antiques and crafts for sale in the surrounding market. With all of these comings and goings, I was very curious why San Bao chose to film two sleeping dogs. I asked him.

"There were two dogs sleeping there. But I filmed them because they had life. They slept there while everything else was going on around them. That was just the point I was trying to capture. Because the dogs just kept sleeping, while other things happened around. To them it did not matter. They were not bothered. But many people come to this place seeking something which is difficult to attain. If they cannot attain what they came to seek, people may not understand the reason why and feel it is strange. I have always had this kind of desire, and during the course of searching for this desire, have been afraid that there will be people who do not understand what I am thinking. For instance, if you do not go out the door for several days, people will think you are strange, because you are different from others. If you are not with people together, people think you are strange because you are different. But if you are with everyone together, everyone will ultimately

35

seek their own rather than be the same as others, but in fact they are really afraid that they will be different from others. This is where the conflict inside lies. But at the same time you must be different from all the others. Character is not something you can find. It is something you cannot find. This comes from the road you have traveled and the things which have become a part of your mind. It is not something you can just find or create, it is a natural expression. In fact, I doubt that very many people will actually go out and search for their own Shangri-la. Most will be just floating without direction or follow the others, not to really go and look."

"Then has the search for Shangri-la just become a fashion, like New Age Music or fusion life style living?"

"Many people will just do what is in fashion," San Bao shrugged. "Not really go to find Shangri-la. For instance the other day a whole bunch of fashion models used Jokhang Temple as a background for their modeling. Why? This is very superficial. This kind of thing disgusts me and I cannot accept it. In fact, it is quite

frightening if you think about it. Real things must be found from within yourself, not just in a place. Not just because you have come to Lhasa you can find it and you cannot find it if you do not come here. The spirit within you is the most important. A monk who wanders begging in the street is looking for something. In fact, he may have already found it. From childhood he may have left home in search of this and in fact this search is Shangri-la. I feel if I search for my own Shangri-la there is still time. When complete, and I look back there should be no regrets. I do not have any thing worth regretting. This life I have lived, as long as it is worth it, then that is good."

"There is a Buddhist concept of a voiceless voice. Can you tell me about soundless sound?"

"I once discussed this in detail with a Buddhist," San Bao replied. "The sound within Buddhism is the most sensitive, as it is the thing one most desires to have, the most basic element of all things. You see I am a composer, so I am most sensitive to sound. This point of

Buddhism is very difficult to understand. When I was young, my teacher taught me something which changed the way I would think ever after. 'You must remember,' he explained, 'within music, the point of silence is actually a part of the music.' My realization suddenly had greater clarity. These words have influenced my own understanding of music ever since."

"So for you, what does Shangri-la mean?"

"One should sometimes just think about what they are doing and consider whether it is worthwhile or not. I often ask myself, what is the meaning of all this, the things I am doing, music I am composing. In this question there is a powerful conflict. I think there are a lot of other things I must still do. When I talk with friends they say when you reach a certain age and you have already done many things and have many accomplishments, you will suddenly wonder and then discover what you really have done, and what you really want to do. My Shangri-la is my own life style. My greatest objective in life is to find Shangri-la, and through my own work it is my search to find and express Shangri-la. But after lots of effort people say such work is not commercial enough. They worry about the market. Actually, I don't care about this. As long as I have created it, then that is alright."

As San Bao explained the vision of his music, I noticed the Mongolian yak hair standard protruding from one of the rooftops of Jokhang Temple, sharp against blue. Golden rooftops with guardian dragons and laughing lions framed Potala Palace in the distance which seemed so close, an illusion arising from clarity of air. We sat on the rooftop of Jokhang Temple all morning, discussing a search for a sound which maybe could not be heard.

The blue sky which stretched behind San Bao in the distance seemed so close that it could be touched at any moment. Just reach out and grab a cloud passing by. Such is illusion perpetuated by the color blue. Such was the clearness of the sky. Awareness undistorted. If Tibetan sky were sound, a chime would ring forever.

## Yak

The yak looks like a great American bison with a water buffalo's head. His body is shaggy and fur flows in a great long mane which gives yak composure of a horse.

The yak is the essential, basic element of sustenance for Tibetan people. They drink yak's milk and yak butter tea, eat yak yogurt and yak milk cheese which can be dried and carried in yak leather bags on horseback for days at a time when nothing else can be eaten. They can also eat yak itself. Yak meat can be air dried, or chopped fresh into fine pieces, wrapped in dumpling shapes and boiled as delicacy. Yak oil burned in lamps is offered in temples or to light one's tent in the dark. Yak fur woven into a tent, is home.

Yak is the single ultimate perpetuator of life for Tibetan nomads. So when a yak dies a solemn moment arises. Tibetan way is to take its skull and present it to a manidui stone altar, or hang it over a door way for protection. This way yak spirit is perpetuated or oversees a passage. A yak can be remembered by praying to its skull. This is a good way to remember someone you care about, but have lost.

During the Yogurt Festival, yaks are decorated as pretty things with *hada* in their horns and flowers in their hair, like little girls preparing for a date, or a Xmas tree about to be lit. Bright saddle blankets with images of lions and dragons are strapped to their backs.

I asked one Tibetan nomad feasting at the Yogurt Festival, "Where is your yak?"

"This is my yak!" he declared pointing to a shaggy hallucination of kaleidoscope colors.

I stared at colors swirling in concentric circles of tinkling bells. "How long did you require in decorating your yak?"

"It took me ten days to completely decorate my yak," he explained. The five colors symbolize elements we live with — water, fire, sky, earth and stone. These elements are always with us."

I wondered how somebody must feel about their yak to dress and make-up a yak like one's daughter about to go for her wedding. So

I asked the nomad how he felt emotionally about his yak. He told me he was in love with his yak. He had raised the yak from a baby. "The yak is always with my family. He is part of our family."

Tassels and bells hang everywhere, from mane, tail and saddle. The tingle of bells is crisp cutting Tibetan air clarity which feels like blue porcelain cracking against the endless chime of bells. I asked about the bells.

"The bells are for protection. They are old, antique, their chime is sweet," explained the nomad. "They have been passed down in our family, from generation to generation, to generation. So when we hear the sound of the bells we hear the same sound our father heard, our grandfather before him, and our great grandfather before him. Can you understand the chime of yak bells?"

In a nomad family, the yaks will be born and die, generation after generation. The family members will be born and die generation after generation. A generation of people and yaks will come and pass, but the bells will be the same. As the nomads wander the bells will travel, across valleys and mountains, across vast space, passages of time. The chime of bells will pass, from generation to generation of both yak and nomad. Yaks and nomads will come and go. Bells remain. Their chime can still be heard.

MANIDUI

# White Eagles

Yang Jin is a Tibetan who moved to Beijing as a child. She cannot speak Tibetan anymore. She has the face of Guanyin, the white version of Green Tara. This shocked me when I first met her. Yang Jin's eyebrows stretched in thin round curves and her eyes evoked a dream of compassion.

Her cousin An Sang is a painter in Tibet. He paints her eyes. Yang Jin said I must find An Sang when I go to Lhasa. So I found An Sang living in a quiet house in a quieter lane. As I stared at his painting of a thousand hand-thousand eye Guanyin, I realized that I was staring at Yang Jin. I wanted to ask him about his paintings. So I asked him about Yang Jin.

"Yang Jin came to Beijing," I asked. "She found a good life there. Have you ever thought about doing the same?"

"Beijing is the capital of China," An Sang explained. "From all materialist aspects, it is very nice. But in Lhasa I can find a feeling. This feeling allows me to paint and there are many things here I can feel. I just walk without direction, look around, and I can see the things I want. Inspiration for my paintings comes from the things I see and feel every day, so I cannot leave these. If I leave this atmosphere, I will leave my inspiration. Therefore, I feel this is a very special place, a place of spirit. I will stay here until I die. As an artist I could not find a better place to be. You see, every person has their own Buddha inside and every person has their own temple palace within. Mine is expressed through my paintings.

42

Therefore, in this place I can paint the things inside my heart."

"You cannot leave here. Is it because you cannot leave Shangri-la?"

"Yes, you can say this. Lhasa, Tibet, this place has not yet been destroyed. It is clean. Here you can see and feel the force of religious inspiration. But in many places, many big cities, this cannot be seen because it has been destroyed. Construction destroys much. In Tibet, you can still see people whose face is pure. From inside a person, you can find that person's value. So, I will definitely stay here."

"Can you explain how you fuse tradition with modern in your painting?" I asked.

"As soon as I went to Tibet University I began to study the painting of traditional Thanka. This is the most delicate and unique painting style of our people. But I cannot just take traditional painting and re-paint it, as my own art is modern. So what I try to do is fuse together the most traditional elements of Tibetan life together with my ideas to create modern art."

An Sang's paintings expressed a sense of solemn power through recurring images, Tibetan women covered in turquoise, thousands of hands and eyes, the unrestrained energy of white eagles. "Can you explain why you have so many white eagles in your paintings?" I asked.

"Once I read about Tibetan sky funerals," he explained. "I was very touched. Buddhism is a person's purity, and ultimate contribution. A Tibetan sky funeral is the most final contribution of a person. You present the meat of your body to wild eagles, and they bring your meat to the temples of heaven. Death becomes an event of life which exceeds reality. So, many of my paintings have images of white eagles which will bring you to another realm. This feeling reminds one that death brings you to the heavenly realm. Tibetans believe only white eagles can really bring your flesh to heaven. So I paint only white eagles. This is a part of human culture.

An Alternative Philosophy Travelogue
White Eagles

43

Many of my art works express something I feel within. My paintings reflect many feelings and inspiration which come from real things and real feelings within. The white eagles of my paintings reflect Tibetan Buddhism. In Tibet there are white eagles and they encircle an altar where corpses are given to eagles. The priests who cut the bodies to prepare the bodies for feeding eagles recognize the eagles and even can call them by name. Moreover, an eagle's dead body cannot be found on the ground because when eagles die they fly to heaven. It is all very clean. In one's mind, we are transposed to heaven."

"Where can we go to watch eagles?"

"In Lhasa, in Ali, there are many places which have altars for presenting human corpses to eagles. When I went to Ali once, I found many spirit mountains along the way. There was a Kampa woman who had died, she was very young. Many Lamas carried her body up to an altar, to present her to eagles. There was nothing on her body. Only eagles eating. I was overwhelmed by a feeling solemn depth. This feeling still overwhelms me to this day. It makes you realize that there are many beautiful things related to life and life style. Therefore, I think that Shangri-la is a palace in another realm, where white spirit eagles, vast nature, all life with great peace, come together in Shangri-la."

"In the Tibetan sky funeral, a person's body completely returns to nature, right?"

"A sky funeral is the funeral style which we Tibetans recognize as the best. Because people are dead, so when you are dead it is best to contribute your flesh to eagles and let them transport you to another place. Of course this is best. Just to let your flesh rot in one place is not as good as letting eagles eat it and transpose it to another realm in the sky. I believe it is a beautiful and natural experience. I believe that Shangri-la is related to this."

"What do you feel when you paint white eagles?"

44

"I feel like I am the eagle's spirit. Or my mother and father, simple pure people. The eagle and our family have no great difference between us. You see, he is quite pure as well."

An Sang went on to explain his other art. He pointed to the painting of a young woman, Guanyin, with the face of his cousin Yang Jin. "The ten thousand-hand and eye Guanyin has many hands to help many people, to help those in difficulty. She has many eyes to see all those in need. This is close to my own beliefs. So I paint these hands and eyes as they have a feeling of order. This is to allow more people to understand and know, because many people still live in poverty, do not have enough to eat or wear, and need the help of others. If more people can help others with pure action, they in turn will be repaid for their purity. A person must study how to be a person. To be a person is to be pure. Religion is one form of purity. Through this, through interaction with all kinds of people, through your own words you can let others know you, as I have let them know me through painting. Through the third eye of Buddha, one can see all the things which man can see, understand others, and understand oneself. Then one will become relaxed, things will come naturally. People's hearts are expressed through one's eyes. Regardless of expression, eyes can express the most. In my heart, the Shangri-la I search for can be sought through the third eye of Buddha."

Tibetan Kampa women, nomads are another favorite theme of An Sang's paintings. "I see that you paint many Kampa women, they exude a feeling of beauty and express power. Can you explain this feeling to me?"

"I like to paint the women of many Tibetan regions. They give one a feeling of tremendous power and greatness. Because if you go to the northern Tibetan grasslands you can see them standing in the freezing cold, many children running about the grasslands without adequate clothing, children of the grasslands. Their life style is actually quite wonderful because the love given to them by their mothers has given me a deep impression. In that harsh and terrible landscape they can raise children to become adults, these women have greatness. I want to express the mother's

45

greatness in the Kampa women of my paintings. They have a Buddha in their heart, and live in the land of spirits. So their eyes are beautiful, like the eyes of a Buddha. In many of my paintings I depict the clothing and jewelry of Tibetan women."

"I see that you put power into the hands and eyes of the women which you paint. Can you tell me the background of clothing you depict in your paintings?"

"From the time I left university I went to the dance troupe and designed stage sets and costumes. Tibetan clothing is special and different from that of other ethnic groups, more colorful. In one small county you can discover many different styles of clothing. You can feel their heart from their clothing. For instance, Tibetan women like to wear very thick necklaces of stone and turquoise.

46

Colors will be in contrast. Their apron will have many contrasting colors as well, like a rainbow. Their hair style is beautiful, they wear precious stones throughout their hair. I want to express many beautiful things in what I paint and present it to everyone. Especially Kampa women, whatever they own, whatever they have, they wear it on their bodies. This time I went to Changdu, for the annual regional art show, and the Kampa women there dressed beautifully. They wore so much jewelry on their bodies that they could not even walk. Several of these women had to be carried onto the stage. Some wore over ten million Renminbi worth of jewels on their bodies. They expressed a feeling inside the Tibetan people, to take the most beautiful things, and bring them to others. Tibetan turquoise and coral these go best with their clothing and fit as jewelry. Therefore, they love nine eye stones. This is to protect them from evil. Tibetans live in a harsh and terrible environment and therefore must protect themselves from the elements. So in my paintings I express this jewelry with the power which it possesses."

"Is Shangri-la here in Tibet?"

"It is said that Tibet is the last place where the environment has not been destroyed and it is where people who love the environment want to protect. Artists should let the world understand the importance of nature, the importance of the environment, of history, of eternal culture. Each person must be responsible to protect these things. My inspiration comes from here. I have gone to many places like Beijing, but I cannot leave this place which is my source. Here I can find the best things inside my heart. Here there is a wonderful religion, and well protected environment. I hope that these things may be kept alive forever. Man and nature should be in balance forever."

"But you haven't answered my question. Where is Shangri-la?"

"It is a beautiful thing, an ideal. It is an ideal in your mind. Every person has a Shangri-la in their heart and mind. In mine I have a Buddha and this is my painting. It is my life style which I love. This is my Shangri-la. Wherever you go to look for Shangri-la it is

47

irrelevant. The most important is your heart, because if you have this inside, you can find Shangri-la wherever you go."

An Sang then spread on his bed designs of different Tibetan clothes which he was working on. Some designs were finished, others still being drawn. These designs were to be used by the Tibetan dance troupe for costumes being manufactured at a factory for disabled Tibetans. The factory only produced Tibetan crafts, clothing, medicinal incense, paper, and other crafts. An Sang offered to take me to the factory if I wanted to visit. So we went.

There were fifty handicapped Tibetans working at a factory called the Lhasa Handicapped Handicraft Centre. Their livelihood was supported by the factory. It was also their home, their social circle, their life. Jampa Tsundhup, the factory director gave them direction, opportunity, hope. When two disabled workers got married, he represented their families as paternal father to both. In many cases the disabled workers did not have any other family members to attend their wedding.

He started the factory with little money, no outside support, no funding from government. In the beginning they had to cook on open fires in the cold of night, as there was no kitchen. Jampa Tsundhup, the factory director, was once a Lama, who left the monastery, discarding his robes, to bring his belief in hope to those who needed it most. He was a Bodhisattva.

In addition to supporting themselves, the fifty disabled workers supported one hundred Tibetan orphan children, many of whom were also disabled. Jampa Tsundhup was also headmaster of Lhasa Jatson Chumig Welfare Special School for the orphans which he had built on the small compound with factory proceeds. They lived in the school and attended classes in Chinese and Tibetan languages. They also sang songs which they wrote. I called San Bao on my mobile and asked him to come over to the school, to listen to their songs. He came immediately. The children were thrilled to see a star like San Bao. They surrounded him. They sang:

"To see a grand eagle, soaring in the sky, you do not know

48

where he is flying

>    Coming to this school, we realize the value of life, wild flowers are blooming...

>    On the first day entering school, half belief half doubt, like a dream...

>    We are grateful for this opportunity in life, it is too sad not to know your own culture...

>    To realize beautiful dreams, please do not pass the good years in vain."

Their song captured stillness in the late Tibetan afternoon when sunlight is strongest and shadows become deep, protruding, abstractions of one's imagination. The sorrow of their condition was drowned in the joy of their singing. They were overcoming predicament.

"Shambhala" is Shangri-la. - - - - - -

# Finding Directions

I telephoned one of the numbers which Douglas Gerber gave me the day I arrived in Lhasa. I spoke to a Tibetan who knew that the living Buddha Vera Ghyentse Rimpoche would be arriving in Lhasa any day. But he was not sure which day, or where he would stay. He suggested that I call one of the other numbers Douglas gave me. Which one? Any one, it did not matter. Just call. If Rimpoche arrives, he will see you.

So I called. I sat on the top floor of a Nepalese café overlooking the square of Jokhang Temple, eating Tibetan *momo* dumplings with *zamba* wheat flour crushed into bread sticks, drinking yak butter tea. When it proved that all of the telephone numbers could not tell me when Rimpoche would arrive or where he would stay, I began to look for him in the cup of yak butter tea. I could not find him. Maybe I was not looking carefully enough.

Then one of his friends arrived in the square looking for me. After several telephone calls we made contact. Yes, Rimpoche had arrived. He had arrived the previous night, but had not told anybody. So he was in Lhasa, but nobody knew except Rimpoche. This was the way Rimpoche preferred to arrive, and leave. This would give him adequate time away from all of those who wanted to follow him, so that he could go alone to Jokhang Temple, light incense and feel the energy projected by hundreds of Tibetan prayer wheels turning clockwise. So if we wanted to find Rimpoche, we should go to Jokhang Temple and look around. We should try to feel the energy and if it is flowing in the right direction, then maybe we can find

Tibet
Lhasa

Rimpoche.

This would require staying at Jokhang Temple, hanging with the monks and feeling the energy. It would require turning off the mobile phone, not making any more calls and listening to chanting of monks without interruption. Imagine, calming one's mind and listening to monks for a few minutes without interruption, even without a mobile phone. It seemed so simple, yet so difficult. I had to imagine. So I stared at the steam rising from a cup of yak butter tea, and smelled the smell of yak. I prepared myself for turning off the mobile phone. Upon pressing the "off" button my mind was transported to a prairie field stretching into the horizon as far as one could stretch the limits of their imagination. At the tip of imagination I could see wild Tibetan ponies running in uncertain directions. I thought about the ponies and wondered what they were looking for. They were running. The direction was uncertain. They just kept running.

This was the point at which I threw my mobile phone into a trash can carefully placed by the Lhasa Municipal Health Department strategically near the Jokhang Temple plaza for the purpose of receiving unwanted scraps of paper, used Kodak film boxes, cigarette butts, and disinherited mobile phones. I went to Jokhang Temple to listen to monks and to find Rimpoche. It was fortunate that I turned off my mobile phone before throwing it in the trash can. Otherwise its ring might upset people passing the trash can who had traveled long distances, searching for something they could not find because their direction was uncertain.

I could not find Rimpoche. We waited at Jokhang Temple. We listened to the sound of monks chanting. We waited. We looked. But we could not find Rimpoche. Suddenly it occurred to me that he might try to call my mobile phone which had been discarded in the trash can so I should try to retrieve the phone. So we went back into Jokhang Temple plaza looking for the mobile phone. It was still in the trash can where I had left it because it did not ring and nobody was disturbed by its presence because I had remembered to turn it off before throwing it into the trash.

You cannot reach it through modern telecommunications, but if you meditate you can go there!

As I dusted off the mobile phone my friend noticed somebody calling us from atop a building in the plaza. He was standing on the balcony of a Tibetan restaurant. The man wore yellow robes of a senior monk. He was waving. It was Rimpoche's assistant. He had found us, we had not found him. I became acutely aware of the fact that we were being found by the person who we wanted to find without finding him or without him finding us, in the complete absence of electronic digitized communication. I suddenly realized that the first step toward finding Shangri-la would begin with the conscious act of throwing out one's mobile telephone. It would be in the process of recovery of something thrown out which we feel is essential but in fact is not, that we realize how important it is to dispossess oneself of those things which we find so convenient.

Rimpoche smiled, as I made my way upstairs to the restaurant balcony. He said hardly anything at all but indicated that he had found me. In fact he had not moved from his seat, eating a bowl of yellow rice the whole time. He had become aware of my frantic search to find him and had asked his assistant to wave to us as we would be looking for a discarded mobile phone at this point in time. Yes, he had gone to Jokhang Temple when we were there, and had left without us knowing. We were looking too hard. Therefore we could not find what we were looking for. So he found us instead.

Rimpoche was born in Lhasa. He started studying Buddhism at age seven. Now he travels the world lecturing and teaching meditation. "I always talk to

52

people in public at universities, and every place I go. I talk of compassion, how to make self peace, peace for others, peace for the environment. People are very interested," he nodded.

"How have you been?" he asked. I told him that I had decided to quit being a lawyer, economist and business advisor to foreign multinational corporations coming to China. I was no longer going to help anyone make money and I was not going to make any myself. At forty-one I had decided to discard the career I had so painfully and carefully built up. I would throw it out like a mobile phone which had been turned off. I was now going through the painful process of disconnecting.

"What are you going to do?" he asked. I told him I was going to produce films about Shangri-la. He thought that this was a good idea and worth pursuing as more people would need to start searching for Shangri-la. The problem would be to find out exactly where Shangri-la was. This process would require more disconnecting. This would be the difficult part. It would require separation of the immaterial from the material, placing the pieces in front of you and understanding which needed to be discarded and which retained. Such a process would require reducing everything down to the essential.

"Materialism will temporarily make you happy," Rimpoche explained. "Money and wealth seem to make peace but usually make more suffering. If you have more materialism, more things to possess, more to take care of, more to desire, you have more suffering. We call it desire. People always look for something because they are not satisfied. Buddhism teaches that you should satisfy yourself, with just enough money, enough things, without pursuing more, then you will be happy, otherwise, you will never be satisfied. Because most people have a material life, they are very busy keeping up with the material. They are stressed and very unhappy. So they ask me how to release the stress through learning Buddhist philosophy and meditation."

Rimpoche never speaks about Buddhism as religion. He refers to it as philosophy. He teaches meditation, not religion. Teaching is a process of learning. "You learn more you want to know more," he explained to me. "It is very deep, very profound. Other religions are also very great but Buddhism always gives the chance to know the answer. Not only say you should believe. You feel is right, you feel satisfied you can start to practise Buddhism. If you do not feel so, there is no need to follow Buddhism. Buddhism gives choice. Buddha said his teaching is like gold. When you buy gold you should test it, put it into fire and test it. If it is enough for your good, for your own benefit, then practise. If not much benefit, just leave like this. Most other religions say you have to follow, you have no choice. Buddhism says up to you, depends on your wish. So when I travel everywhere many people ask questions. I gave them the answers, most people are happy."

So I took the opportunity to ask a question. "Where is Shangri-la?"

"The search for Shangri-la is not new," Rimpoche explained. "Many had tried to follow this road before, most got lost. In the years between 1962 up until around 1973, lots of people in Europe and America were taking drugs for happiness but most of them were not happy. Some people even died from drugs. I helped people to stops drugs, to make peace. At that time most people are drug people. Now in these days it is not the same, all ages, young age, everybody is looking for peace, happiness. Begin with doing social work to help people. In east Tibet and Qinghai many people have problems — sickness, no education, no medicine, they have much suffering. So I am going to give them education. I started a school and this year a clinic. There are monks and nuns who want to practice, I also give them teaching. And also social work, I did help them to build three bridges. I help poor people many are old age, young children without education. I am happy to do this, apart from religion. People become very happy. I hope in the future I can do more to help people. Yes, it is much work to do."

I told him I was on my way to Qinghai. "Traveling is dangerous," he explained with a word of caution. "Most difficult is in Qinghai.

One must travel many days by car, by jeep. One day my car fell down off the road, I did not die but the car was damaged," he shrugged matter of fact. "Lhasa is my home," explained Rimpoche. "Every time I traveled, I came back here. I remember I was six years old when I was here. There were 200 Lamas together here. I came to join the Lamas." The sound of 200 lamas chanting overwhelmed my mind like a rush of waves over rocks which would disappear amidst the sound of waves. Then the sound of Lamas vanished and I felt silence, the sound of one's mind going blank but becoming clear, against the pulse of heart beating through one's mind like a fat red drum.

Rimpoche could see this in the back of my mind like looking at a mirror from behind its reflection against the light of another mirror from which a candle burned with the anticipation of wax melting shortly, but not as quickly as one might expect. "Lhasa is still the center of Tibet and Shangri-la," he interrupted my thought. The fat red drum stopped beating, for just a moment. So if Lhasa is Shangri-la, then the search for Shangri-la could end where it had begun?

Rimpoche explained that according to Tibetan philosophy the world is now in age of Kali, a time of seemingly endless war, pestilence and suffering. This period would one day be followed by the future. "Shambhala is Shangri-la," Rimpoche explained. "Shambhala is the future king. There is suffering and peace. There are four continents. South, east, west, Shangri-la is the north continent. It exists but you can not reach there. In this world we have many disasters, much fighting. In Shangri-la we all look for something else, a future continent, time of peace. I think they are looking for future. Some call it Shambhala, others Shangri-la, very popular, because this is the future in another world. Now the world is small because of modern communication. But Shangri-la can not be reached through telecommunication. If you practise meditation you can reach Shangri-la." That was all he said. He stood up slowly, then left. The monks in attendance, silent throughout our conversation, followed. As saffron robes brushed past, Rimpoche left as he arrived, unexpected.

55

# Departure

The main street around Jokhang Temple is shaped like a Chinese octagon. So if one flew above the Jokahang Temple like a bird and looked below, you would find a great Chinese octagon with the temple in center like a yin-yang. Energy emanates from the temple. It circles like many people in the street outside, turning wheels. The wheels turn, and with them a concentric energy, which seems to draw endless numbers of Tibetans to the temple on their pilgrimage to turn prayer wheels.

Behind the Jokhang Temple there is an Internet bar. It is called the Yellow Room. Actually it was a secret palace of the Sixth Dalai Lama. He used to come to the Yellow Room to find quiet and write poetry. Now the Yellow Room is an Internet bar. Young travelers come here to drink chai masala Indian milk tea, eat banana pancakes, and get on line.

A girl with purple hair and silver Tibetan bracelets on her wrists, running up both arms to elbow came down the stairway from a rooftop garden of the Yellow Room, where she had been sitting in afternoon shadows looking for Shangri-la in a cup of chai masala. She flipped on a computer and began to surf the web. I asked her where she was from and whether she could help me send an e-mail to a friend.

"You're from Guangzhou?"

"Yes, I am from Guangzhou."

"How long have you been here?"

56

"Hmm. I think two weeks. No, already sixteen days."

"Sixteen days? Why did you leave such a developed and wealthy city as Guangzhou where you have everything you want? Just leave Guangzhou and come to Lhasa?"

"How can I answer? Because I am studying film making. So I thought Lhasa is a good place to make a film. One day maybe I will make such a film. This is only one reason. In addition, there is another reason. Lhasa is mysterious, exuding with religious color. I came carrying what I believed packed in my baggage. Maybe I will leave without my baggage. Maybe I am a Buddhist in disguise."

"Guangzhou is such a developed place, a modern city. A materialist place, I can't understand why you came here?"

"Guangzhou is too noisy and crass. Life there is too fast, competition fierce. So the people have become noisy and crass."

"So you came here looking for something?"

"Yes, I came looking for some spirit."

"I see that you collect a lot of Tibetan jewelry."

"I like these kinds of arts things, yah know."

"This is chic, new fashion."

"This is new fashion? I don't reckon so. It's just what I like. I like to collect Tibetan things. By the way, getting on the internet is slow. It may still take a while. What do you want to write in this e-mail."

"Write to aijing@aijing.com. Just say 'I am in Lhasa, but I still cannot find Shangri-la.'"

"That's it?"

"That's it."

"Ok. I understand. By the way, I don't think you can find Shangri-la in Lhasa."

"Why?"

"Because the Lhasa my friends told me about, is already not like what they told me about. It is not the way it should be. It is already too commercialized. You have to go to Namutsuo Lake, a more difficult place to go than here. There at Namutsuo you feel the real depth. You may find what you are looking for."

"So if one wants to find Shangri-la, one should leave Lhasa and travel to Namutsuo Lake. Is that what you're saying?"

"Namutsuo is really beautiful, a good place to shoot a film."

"Really? Then are you saying that I should go to Namutsuo Lake?"

"Yeah, but not necessarily. This depends on whether the lake calls you to go. If it calls, then go."

I went. On the way I found a pile of stone. What moves a stone, wind, rain, sand, or a bigger stone?

The Tibetans pray to nature. A *manidui* is made of stones piled one on top of another, covered with *jingfan* prayer flags. These stone piles will be placed upon different centers of energy. *Jingfan* prayer flags may be draped across a road, an important shrine, a point of departure.

Sometimes a yak's skull is placed upon *manidui* pile of stones, usually with care and attention, without moving a single stone. The yak's skull may be picked clean by eagles, its bone whitened

Wild Horses
Running in uncertain
Directions . . . .

Tibet

Namutsuo Lake

spirit on white horse

58

by the wind and sun.

A *manidui* is a good place to come alone, to sit and watch a stone and ask oneself how long the stone has been left untouched, unbothered. Is the placing of stones upon a *manidui* part of a design, a plan? Were stones intentionally placed here to be found by someone else? Whose hand placed the stones? Were the hands which placed the stone carved of wind, dust and stone? In the relationship between a hand and a stone, the space for margin of error is impossible. Intention is deliberate.

On the road to Namutsuo Lake, one is reminded to stop at a *manidui* wrapped in white *hada* scarves and colorful *jingfan*. One knows that this is the correct *manidui* because upon reaching this place you will have a sense of departure.

Finding the *manidui* is not difficult. One must look for a place before snow-capped mountains, where energy is emitted from the skull of a yak which still has mats of black yak hair attached to meat which eagles have forgotten to strip clean, or left behind for some unexplained reason. If one needs to know a reason, ask the eagles. High monks at sky funeral altars can call them by name. So can you.

You may try to have a conversation with the yak's skull. Dialogue may be difficult. He will laugh at you and the eagles will fly away in distress. At this point you will become acutely aware that there is no heaven above. There is no hell below. There is nothing behind and nothing in front. At this point, the indicators are pointing in parallel direction. By thinking you had reached the end of the road, it is only a point of departure from the beginning of where you have been. Now your senses can be clear. There is only one direction. Continue.

Behind the *manidui* there is a range of snow-capped mountains, lost in mist, sometimes rain. Above the rain there is snow. The Tibetans say that amidst the snow at a point roughly 5 000 meters above sea level, there is a palace of snow which cannot be found because the place is too cold and far away to search for. The palace is home of Nianjia Tangle, protector of nomads, sheep and yak. The protector spirit lives in the palace of snow. He rides a stunningly beautiful white horse. The mane is fine, like snow.

59

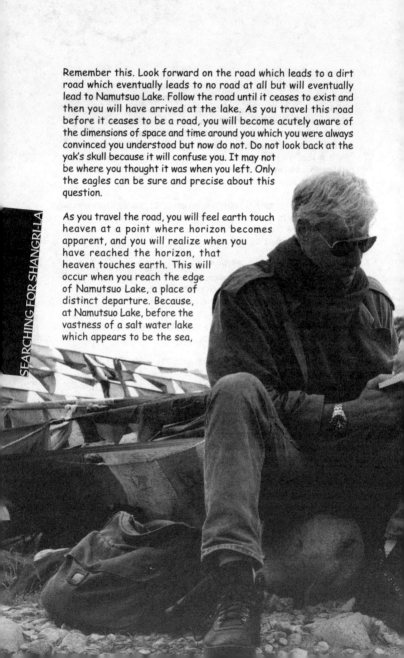

Remember this. Look forward on the road which leads to a dirt road which eventually leads to no road at all but will eventually lead to Namutsuo Lake. Follow the road until it ceases to exist and then you will have arrived at the lake. As you travel this road before it ceases to be a road, you will become acutely aware of the dimensions of space and time around you which you were always convinced you understood but now do not. Do not look back at the yak's skull because it will confuse you. It may not be where you thought it was when you left. Only the eagles can be sure and precise about this question.

As you travel the road, you will feel earth touch heaven at a point where horizon becomes apparent, and you will realize when you have reached the horizon, that heaven touches earth. This will occur when you reach the edge of Namutsuo Lake, a place of distinct departure. Because, at Namutsuo Lake, before the vastness of a salt water lake which appears to be the sea, realization occurs that you cannot go further.

Before snow-capped mountains, pray for protection from the spirit on a white horse. Rains will arrive. They will cover the mountain from view, and then they too will disappear. If you see a rainbow, you may mistake it for a spirit on a white horse. He has already come and gone too. If you hear thunder, listen without fear. It is only a resounding voice of protection. The echo is your own thoughts standing on Tibetan plateau grassland full of flowers in the rain, clapping your hands alone. If you do not pay attention, the rainbow will also soon be gone. So do not stop looking for the spirit on a white horse. He will eventually arrive. Just wait. Close your eyes. Remember. Do not let the altitude disorient you. Confusion is unnecessary.

This means that you cannot stay here very long but should leave a prayer tied to a white *hada* scarf tied to a rock tied to this place. You must then leave immediately. Do not look back.

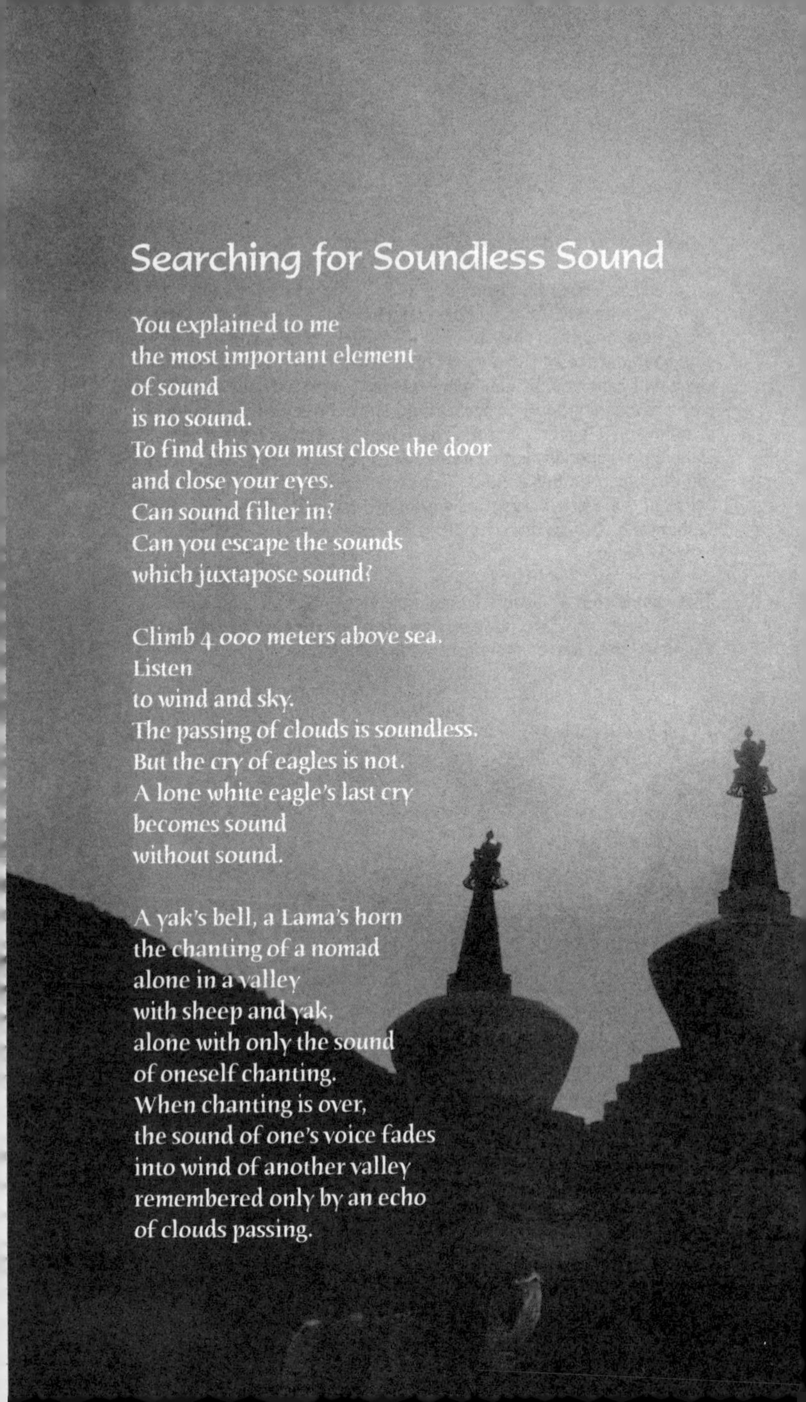

# Searching for Soundless Sound

You explained to me
the most important element
of sound
is no sound.
To find this you must close the door
and close your eyes.
Can sound filter in?
Can you escape the sounds
which juxtapose sound?

Climb 4 000 meters above sea.
Listen
to wind and sky.
The passing of clouds is soundless.
But the cry of eagles is not.
A lone white eagle's last cry
becomes sound
without sound.

A yak's bell, a Lama's horn
the chanting of a nomad
alone in a valley
with sheep and yak,
alone with only the sound
of oneself chanting.
When chanting is over,
the sound of one's voice fades
into wind of another valley
remembered only by an echo
of clouds passing.

QINGHAI

 Connecting with a Stone

After leaving Tibet, I traveled to Qinghai. The road was long, and I often slept on the back seat of trucks or jeeps. I was lucky enough to flag down with my thumb. Drivers were not used to stopping for hitchhikers, especially a foreign one. But some stopped, partly out of interest, partly for amusement. One old driver kept practicing his English with me the whole time, the whole long road. I could not sleep. I could not think. I could not look out the window at what was passing by. He just kept speaking English at me. Finally, I got off and just walked.

The summer sky was pristine blue, an occasional white cloud passed overhead. The road stretched across rock, mountain platitudes of grassland, expanses of one's mind unfolding like waves churning in a vast sea of space which has not been limited by design or structure. I followed this process of deconstruction. The road led somewhere, but it was in the inconclusiveness of not being sure where that somewhere would lead, that the road became worth following. So I followed.

I must have been hitchhiking and was probably dumped off by one jeep or a truck, and before I could find the other I wandered somewhere which was really nowhere in particular until I came upon a tea shop, the kind which sells nothing much except tea, yak butter tea. I stopped to have a cup and a girl walked in and sat behind me. She was covered with Tibetan turquoise, but I knew right away she was not Tibetan. She wore a bandanna around her head and huge earrings. But I knew from her composure that she

64

was not a nomad. Was she a gypsy in disguise?

It was the fashion designer Flora Cheong-leen, known throughout China as Zhang Tianai. A friend I had known from my years in Hong Kong and Beijing, I did not expect to find her here, collecting turquoise and Tibetan weavings. She too was traveling throughout western China, searching for elements to inspire new fashion designs in elements of Shangri-la.

Flora Cheong-leen, fashion diva, famous designer, brand, label, an image in up-end shopping malls covered with white marble, the kind you can see your reflection in when there are not too many people walking or can slide across when wearing Bally shoes after the janitor in white starched janitor shirt has mopped the white marble white. I stared at my reflection in white yak butter and pretended it was the fancy marble floor of just one of those shopping malls which has covered in quick drying cement the old crippled ancient alleyways of Beijing which I liked to wander through on an autumn day when leaves had already turned gold but were not yet dry enough to fall into and be carried dreamlike, by wind.

It was a rainy late summer day, the kind one wants to be sitting in a Tibetan tea house, drinking yak butter tea. Just one of those yak butter tea days, the kind which leaves one sitting at an old wooden table, looking out the window, counting rain drops. I counted. Flora counted too. Then we began to talk, after we ran out of rain drops.

After staring at my slowly expanding raindrop in a flat surface of yak butter tea which one could pretend was an up-end shopping mall on anything other than a rainy day, I finally asked Flora why Tibetan chic was now becoming chic everywhere else except in Tibet. "People are looking for what is next in fashion," she explained. "Fashion started from Paris. The French wanted to look like Italians and the Italians like Americans and the Americans like British, we then had the prep look. It is all hollow, no substance. You don't dress like a nun because you believe in Catholicism. Everything depends on economy and politics. Look at the politics. Can you trust anything, Enron, accountants, war on the horizon? Look at China, a five thousand year history. This history gives people a secure feeling because it has lasted so long. So what if China has gone up and down and up and down? The fact that it has lasted so long, makes people feel good to just know that."

"So, then what you're really saying is this new ethnic Shangri-la style is not a fad but a reaction against the globalization movement of the 1990s which many associate with ultra-materialist values?" I took a sip of hot yak butter tea, tried to swallow what I had just said.

"It is not just a reaction because I think people today are really lost. People are saying, 'Hey look, I am swimming around in all of this materialism. I have black pants, blue pants, white pants and all of these things and look like a robot.' This robot like outfit system gives me no security. At the same time western material values are messing with a lot of global people, threatening their ethnicity, the things which give one identity, a sense of security. They don't understand what's really happening, so they react through dress. The combination of colors and beads, mixing old stuff with new stuff, are things which make them feel fulfilled, evidence that

66

some things have continued and lasted so long."

"But in many ways it seems that Chinese ethnic chic is being re-imported back into China after becoming accepted as vogue in Paris and Milan," I pressed Flora's views.

"In Milan and Paris they set the standards. Asia follows the west. China has just opened up only over the past few years, so they think, what I have is no good. It is nothing," Flora picked up a piece of traditional ethnic brocade she had been thumbing on the table and held it forward for me to touch. "This has been going on for ages and ages in the streets of China. Crochet for table cloth or anything. All these big magazines and American media are now just putting it into the mainstream. Promotion is making it come back from the darkness of forgotten tradition. Media has all the control and they can import anything. Chinese have always had it, but it does not have value to them because it does not have a brand name on it. So they create a brand look-a-like. They need that identity."

Flora then took a sip of yak butter tea and thought about what she had just said. Fingering a string of Tibetan corals which I knew she was imagining could be repackaged with a touch of something else and turned into Fifth Avenue fashion with a price tag to reflect the rent. "About the west using our ethnic traditional things," she went on staring into her cup of yak butter tea, "I think it is very simple, they have run out of their own stuff. Pop, fast-food life style packaged in a can is just not enough. It lacks emotion and moreover, most of the people have not traveled out of their own realm, so they do not

67

know anything else. Look, 80% of Americans don't even have a passport! So when you present these people with Asian ethnic, they are shocked, and at the same time stimulated by it. Even people from other parts of Asia, say Singapore, they have not been to these places, so they are stimulated by it too. Meanwhile the media promotes it. The west promotes it. Armani and Gucci are now using ethnic things because they are somebody. So they think it is a western thing." She then looked into her cup of yak butter tea. She looked carefully. "Where does tea come from? How is water transcended into our cup? We people come from somewhere. This is our soul. Designing is thinking. Things come from here. The west is doing ethnic things, so suddenly ethnic fashion comes from there. But if you go back a long time, these things come from China."

"Then Chinese or ethnic Shangri-la chic is a fusion of east-meets-west style plus values. Or am I missing something?"

"A lot of Asian and western designs use the actual product, say antique patches. They go and look for some ethnic driven handcraft, merge it on the clothes, such style is popular. A lot of designers in Europe and America are putting folklore craft look into their clothes. I am different. People like comfort. Maybe, because I myself am ethnic, Chinese, a dancer, a sportswoman, I design what suits my life style best. The design of my pants is big bell bottoms, low hips because the future is driven by natural sexuality. I put patches of Chinese ethnic fabrics and Tibetan leather to impact. Life is nothing but clashes and how you render them. There is no east meets west. With my combination I am very western, very Chinese, and very futuristic, it is a snow mountain, my state of mind and life, future is fusion, if you do not fuse there is no future. If you are single minded isolated in a bottom of a well, you are isolated, you must fuse in culture, in people. Remember, there are no boundaries."

"Then for you Flora, returning to China, traveling to these isolated areas, is in a way a search for your own ethnicity. Yeah?"

"When I did costumes at the Royal Ballet, I realized the future is

68

only what people tell you. You go to a design school, graduate, and they tell you you're a great designer. Why? They told you sleeves are like this and there are so many sleeves. But in fact, they come from somewhere. Everything comes from somewhere. Food comes from somewhere. A buffet comes from somewhere. Fusion food, sushi and noodles all come from something. Nobody ever asks. People are born in a place. So I began exploring my roots which brought me back to China. I had forgotten living in the west that I was Chinese. Now I am back in China. I have no choice. All things have a connection with how the ethnic groups called for rain and life, hope in search of heaven, in search of something. That is where movements start from energy connecting from the dantian, my energy transcends to you to everyone."

"Then people are searching for something else, something beyond. They are just disillusioned. Right?" I looked into my cup of yak butter tea searching for disillusionment.

"People need much more space for illusion and hope. Western people's life is a repeat of everything, the same street corner, same fashion shop, just the same. Western culture has created a world of material repeat, brand logo. People live with stereotype. So everyone is coming here in search of something, not just tangible materialism. This is an era of change. Asians have it, but cannot see it. They have thousands of years of thinking but they do not want to see it, only concrete jungles. They see repeated brand names and want to look like everybody else. They are in fact lost."

"Then it is a rejection of the material, realization that materialism can only bring you so far? But haven't you been accused by Hong Kong paparazzi of being a material girl?"

"I can shamefully say I have everything under the sun from houses, cars, friends, power, money, fame. It's shameful, because when I go home I realize it is all superficial. All this materialism is not constructive." Showing me a Tibetan necklace she had collected, Flora pointed to the crude uncut raw turquoise stones with her fine fingernail. "This is not a diamond. But these are real stones.

69

Since I have been meditating, traveling around China and visiting beautiful mountains, this is what gives me security because this has energy, earth power. Vibrant energy gives me security because I feel connected and this brings me in balance. It has nothing to do with city values. So what if I have a diamond ring worth thousands of dollars and wear it on the street and everyone looks at me and says 'wow she's rich'. So what? It just cheapens me. I feel raped. My values have now changed."

Flora then carefully laid all of the Tibetan turquoise rings and things she had been collecting that week on the rough wooden table for me to look at. We looked at each piece, emanating with energy of mountains from which it had come. "Look at these people," Flora pointed out the window at Tibetans passing in the rain, their faces are covered with colorful cloth bandannas. "They have been riding horses, on the planes, eating natural food, that is how life should be and that is how god made us. We've been putting ourselves into a dark hole into a prison, where we have to manufacture everything. Sometimes we manufacture and design so much of our lives that we are just ruining everything in the end. For some searching for Shangri-la is a reaction to the cycle. For others, they do not know where they are going so they are hoping to connect with something through the process of searching."

"Then how does one connect to a stone?" I asked.

"Natural stone is becoming an important part of everyone's life, whether in chandeliers, jewelry, or furniture. Stone is metaphysical, spiritual, and physical. When you see stones you feel good, their colors embody all the elements. And when you are alone you feel the energy setting into you connecting through visual beauty. It is a philosophy you believe in. The stone has energy. So we realize that we must connect ourselves, otherwise we will not be connected to a piece of stone. I would rather be seen in this," she picked up a Tibetan silver ring inlaid with chunks of rough turquoise and coral, "than some million dollar diamonds where it is like a brand name. Diamonds are forever. I do not want to belong to that philosophy at all anymore, live this life of brands and money. My values have changed."

"You built an entire fashion brand 'Tian Art' around the concept of integrating China's traditional 'five elements' and juxtaposing their colors. Why have you embraced the five elements as part of your own philosophy?"

"My five elements in clothes have all the colors of the five elements of Chinese tradition: gold, fire, earth, water and wood. I want to make clothes for people who will feel the elements themselves internally, help them feel emotional balance, without which you too will be in a state of turmoil all the time. Remember, the elements are first physical, then emotional, last spiritual. Without that extra energy you cannot live modern life. So you have to get that spirituality. Go to Tibet first, get spiritual then the physical and emotional will follow. Remember, don't get mental. All this mental state fixes people in a hierarchy where they are condemning, and judgmental, becoming unnecessarily political. Then it upsets everything."

"Then it is the spiritual which you are seeking here?"

"Most important are spiritual beliefs because ultimately I will leave the earth when I get old. Imagine saying to one's kid, 'Darling, mommy is dying but you must have a big house. If I leave you with this big house, you have to do things in this big house. If I leave you with a million dollars you have to spend it.' Do you think life will at all be easy for them? Life is how you live it. This material life style is now a religion and money is a fixation that is actually harming everyone everywhere without knowing. Ruthlessly, without boundaries or edge, people's attitude is for money I will do anything. So now I travel, to mountains, rivers, the western part of China, go north, it's all about different emotions, feelings, culture, which really enforces our natural goodness, rather than manufactured things."

"So Flora, tell me, what are you really doing here?" I took another sip of yak butter tea and felt its warmth circulate within against the cool late summer rain beating on the edge of outside window. "Don't tell me you are also searching for Shangri-la."

71

"I come here for Zen. Peace of mind. It is power of feelings and power of peace over one's mind. A natural connection to the land makes me feel power. Having a natural connection with heaven, water, woods, trees, I am in heaven because I am the happiest that way. When I first saw the movie about Shangri-la, Lost Horizon, thousands of years of living and feeling happy, I think heaven is like that. I was brought up believing in heaven and hell. But that's lateral. Searching for Shangri-la goes beyond searching for Shangri-la. This is because Shangri-la is a place beyond a place, beyond horizontal. When you close your eyes you can think about it any way and that is Shangri-la. It is the security of your energy, soul, balance, without any dependence on anyone, your boss, your husband, your lover, your clothing, your material satisfaction. I can have a glass of water and a bowl of rice and be happy. That is my Shangri-la."

"What about the search for Shangri-la?"

"The search for Shangri-la for me is all about intention in my mind. I am referring to good, positive intention. I live a fusion life style. There are no clashes for me between regions, cultures and people. This comes with connecting the past with present, through traveling, experiencing everything. If you do not experience you cannot fuse because you will be stuck with limited vocabulary. People and culture must fuse, only then you can find Shangri-la. You must search without searching, but you cannot search without knowledge. Maybe for some people, if you are gifted, you can search while you are looking in Tibet and Yunnan. But sometimes it just comes only before you die, or maybe with lightning with thunder, maybe back in your office in the most materialistic period of your life. Like a fever you overcome and wake up. It can be caused by anything. But the most important is connection."

"Am I taking the right road to Shangri-la?"

"Connection is a point. Tibet is a point. But to say I have been there and now I am holistic is just hearsay. Everyone has their own story and own journey. You will find many, many people and levels. It all depends on who you meet. There are thousands of

levels of connection, don't ever forget this. Remember, it is a long, long road, you are about to take, and it is at that level, which you must connect."

Flora then looked out the window. The rain drops were still falling. Tibetan nomads passed outside, their faces wrapped in colorful bandanas, chunks of raw turquoise sewn into their hair. Only black forlorn eyes peered from behind the bandanas wrapped across their face. Flora nodded toward the nomads, gypsies.

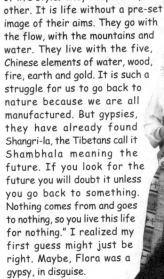

"The life style of gypsies is very good. They are connected with heaven and earth. They can live anywhere. They have no set form of life style. They keep warm, comfort and are happy with each other. It is life without a pre-set image of their aims. They go with the flow, with the mountains and water. They live with the five, Chinese elements of water, wood, fire, earth and gold. It is such a struggle for us to go back to nature because we are all manufactured. But gypsies, they have already found Shangri-la, the Tibetans call it Shambhala meaning the future. If you look for the future you will doubt it unless you go back to something. Nothing comes from and goes to nothing, so you live this life for nothing." I realized my first guess might just be right. Maybe, Flora was a gypsy, in disguise.

Flora Cheony-Teen says "throw out diamonds & wear torn jeans!"

73

# Nothing Left

Qinghai. I was searching for nomads. They are hard to find. Being nomads, they move all the time, changing their place. They move like wind. You cannot keep up. When you try to find them, they disperse. To find them is difficult. This is because you must concentrate on dispersion.

To find nomads, you must follow a road which leads in no particular direction and keep following it. The problem is that nomads keep a distance from roads. They travel where there are no roads. This is what differentiates them from us. It is what makes them nomads.

To find the exact location of nomads will require a tool. Neither a compass nor map will do. This involves a ball of string. It is quite difficult for most people to imagine how a ball of string will help. But it is actually quite simple. To find nomads, requires, unraveling a ball of string.

A ball of string is string wrapped around crossing itself from different directions until it becomes a hard ball of tight amassed string without discernable end. A ball of string is very tight. It provides no space for flexibility. It is a completely solid mass of something which in fact has no solid foundation. It is only because

it has been interwoven over itself, logically and systematically wrapped and twisted upon its own internal emptiness that the string can exist in its own self-paralyzing state. This is the state of twisted string.

A mind can be twisted string. So can a body. So hold a ball of twisted string aloft in the air and pretend that a kite has been attached to the string and this kite is an eagle, carried aloft by air in concentric waves under its wings. The ball of string will unravel. There will be a momentary feeling of anticipation that all which has been so carefully wrapped will soon be undone, that careful and logical process of creating a tight ball of string may be unwoven or dismantled. This idea can threaten one's instincts, and place them off guard. But in process of unraveling comes the freedom of unwrapping something which deserves to be freed. In fact, it was meant to be undone.

From this point you can begin to understand the rationale of following a road into Qinghai which leads nowhere at all. Qinghai means "green sea" in Chinese. It is a green sea. In all four directions the land is green. There are green hills and mountains, green rivers and lakes, green reflected in a blue sky. Stand in the green and look up at the blue sky and twist your body in concentric circles in any direction you choose but do not move your position to either the left or right of center. After a while you will feel completely dizzy. Then sit down and look at the hills around you. They will encircle you like horses on a merry-go-round except that they are green and they do not end when the dizziness does. This is how one enters Qinghai.

Now take your life into your hands for a second by standing on a rock and looking out over a canyon where there are no single signs of any person existing for as far as you can see or hear. This canyon exists in Qinghai. You may not believe that it exists or is as big as the Grand Canyon in Arizona which is flooded by hundreds of tourists every day and has a special national park service center to make sure that you do not feed the grizzly bears or hike in places where rattlesnakes prefer to sleep during the afternoon to

avoid sun. But the canyon in Qinghai is somehow every bit as big and deep. There are only two differences. The first is that because there are no tourists, there is no need for tourist hosting service centers. In fact there are no people at all. The second, if you try to reach high enough without falling off of the rocks, you can almost touch eagles. The eagles are white.

At this place if you listen one can hear only wind. Wind eliminates other sounds in your mind, rushing through conscious like a rising tide which suddenly subsides, leaving waves to crash upon rocks. When you feel the white salt water breaking about, open your eyes and realize for a second that you are nowhere near the sea but standing on a cliff far above the Yellow River which runs below. The sound of waves was only an illusion. It was just the breathing of eagles.

Place a call on a mobile phone where connection still can be obtained upon a cliff where the Tibetans have left stones and prayer flags, a small *manidui* reachable only by a hike over a thin ridge from which if you fall, there will be no return, except to be washed into the brown rich sticky mud of the Yellow River, from this point is only a thin snake-like line twisting below. Place a call by satellite signal and hold the phone up as high as you can, into the wind. Remember not to lose your balance. Let somebody somewhere else who will never have the opportunity to visit this canyon because they will never leave their glass and steel office tower, listen to the wind in this place without people, and try to understand the reason why white eagles cry after eating fresh blood. If they hang up the phone on you, just hike on.

This brings us back to the question of the ball of string. Start to unravel it. Pull the string along with you. Watch it unravel. There is a road which you can see as far as you can see and when you turn your head you can only see what you left behind as far as you can remember. When you forget what you remembered, you may begin again. This is the paradox you will find yourself in throughout a journey down this road into the place called green sea. Now imagine the ball being unraveled in your hand during the course of this

77

journey. Imagine that you keep pulling the string and the ball turns around in concentric, consecutive circles. As the string gets longer, the ball gets smaller. By progressing in a process toward infinity, it will eventually disappear.

Now begin the same process. Follow the road as it passes villages which are simple. In the eyes of some they may be poor, in the eyes of others rich. Hitchhike by placing a thumb up in the wind. The trucks will pass. There are only trucks on this road, large transport vehicles, blue steel iron trucks filled with horses, sheep, people, Tibetans and Muslims with bandannas covering their faces from sun and dirt, revealing only black eyes staring back with an empty forlorn feeling one gets from traveling for many days on a single dirt road.

The trucks pass quickly spraying mud. The mud spatters on your jeans. Do not mind. As far as they are concerned, you were not meant to be here, so they ignore you. Then the trucks are gone until more trucks arrive only to pass without stopping. Keep hitchhiking in rain and wind. As wind blows rain, clouds pass revealing snow capped mountains, from which snow melts into water which trickles into rivers which roar in the direction you wish to proceed in. Follow the rivers and they will lead you. Listen to the sound of ice dissipating upon stone becoming water which is ice cold. Look for signs of white eagles.

The rivers lead into more mountains. There are canyons like Sedona, Bryce Canyon, places like this which you have passed in another lifetime in southwestern Arizona or New Mexico. The feeling of hitchhiking is the same. A truck passes, one stops. You hop in and travel to the next point of arrival which becomes a point of departure. Then walk until you are tired, rest. The space is a sequence of layers through time. Time becomes elusive like white eagles, flying close but never forgetting to stop. They too are afraid of losing their balance.

This is a place where desert is surrounded by snowcapped distant mountains, in your mind Shangri-la. Only in Qinghai do you see such

a contrast, white snow capped mountains which can only be reached through hiking across white dunes of sand, which cannot be crossed. This means that the mountains are unreachable. No such place ever existed in your mind. So you believe it must be an illusion. You try to convince yourself of this point. You even insist, because you have run out of string.

Before reaching sand dunes, a young Tibetan girl runs with her sheep. Behind, her long hair is braided into a pattern of turquoise which is her greatest material possession. She wears it in her hair while tending sheep before sunset. She forgets it is there, or that such turquoise weighs heavy on the back of her head. In fact, it does not bother her at all, because she already disregarded possession. As she runs quickly through the grasslands, the sheep scatter. They run in different directions.

If you dare to cross dunes, cover your face with a bandanna. The sun will scorch you here and make your head throb with pain of sharp penetration burning into your mind. The mirage which you see is only your own shadow in cracking alkaline on a road which runs through desert. This is where you come in the late afternoon, to sit and watch your shadow grow, stretch into the horizon, and disintegrate before you.

There are faint contours in the land which give way to more patches of grass and Tibetan nomads herd sheep. Faces covered in colorful bandanas, they are gypsies. Turquoise sewn into hair, trails across the shoulders of young women. They are herding sheep. Ask them where Shangri-la is. They will laugh at you. They hurry to round up more sheep before sunset. If you wait, you may be left where they left you, asking the same question.

Cross sand dunes. They will lead where you do not want to go, but must. It is part of the journey that will only end in the early morning hours when a pick-up truck brings you to a Muslim village. The men sit in a broken wooden shop drinking eight treasure tea, made of rock sugar and dates. The men talk, sometimes laugh. Hot lamb is served with noodles cut with a long wide knife. It is a Muslim village,

An Alternative Philosophy Travelogue
Nothing Left

79

so no liquor is served. Everyone drinks tea. A dog barks somewhere, another howls. Their cry is soon forgotten.

The pick-up truck continues. It will eventually bring you through dark of night to a town, which you will not discover until dawn. When you awake on a bed above a shop house where some monks led you in your sleep, when the truck dumped you along the road. It is a cowboy town. The Tibetans come here in boots and high hats. Some ride motorcycles. They push their way into Muslim restaurants and order racks of fresh lamb. The lamb is killed outside, nearby. Muslims pray when they kill a lamb, because its screams can be disturbing. Here in mountains air is cold all year. They eat a lot of lamb. Prayers of deference are continuously given.

Leave the restaurant. They will sweep the lamb bones onto the floor and then serve more lamb, followed by eight treasure tea. More prayers will be given. But you will not be there to listen, because, you will have already entered the mountains.

A woman enters the restaurant as you leave. She is wrapped in blankets, a tall felt

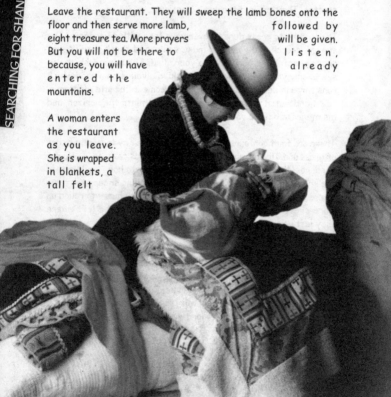

hat upon her head. She has high red-burned Tibetan cheeks, a forlorn smile of hopeless graciousness. Her hands are already tough as leather but her face is soft as the child in her hands. She pulls it close to her breast for feeding. She is young. It is her first baby. She holds this child as if it is the only thing she will ever have. It is.

The mountains lead to a place where green becomes layers of dry earth. Upon which grows sparse grass, long grass, stretching into planes. The planes rise in plateaus. There are ridges, layers of dirt which show disintegration by wind. The wind was here first. You cannot keep up with it. If you try to catch wind, it will behave elusive, and mislead you into following dust blowing in all directions.

There are spots of alkaline on the plane, parched scabs where dryness has sucked sweet water from earth, drawing salt-like alkaline to surfaces forming flat white patches. The earth here is cracked like a jigsaw puzzle somebody forgot to put together. In frustration they left wandering off into the desert to die.

Such sense of sudden desertion haunts patches of alkaline. Watch your shadow in those broken pieces of flat ground. They will cause an illusion and you will believe that your entire image is a shattered mirror reflecting something which you do not want to imagine but which has already happened and passed before you as a subconscious image.

When your own image has shattered between stark lines of cracked alkaline earth, you will see this reflected mood of your soul. Stand up and walk away. It is time for you to walk into the desert as well.

Now it is time for you to walk into the desert

81

# Finding Nomads

I did not find the nomads. When time was appropriate, they found me. They knew it was the appropriate time, because, I had already entered the mountains.

At 4 000 meters above sea level, the road ceases to exist. It becomes a walking trail, then a path, then a creek. After crossing the creek, I came upon prints of horse hooves in mud. I stepped across mud. The creek led into a valley. There were three Tibetan pagodas in the valley with some *jingfan* tied to them. There was nothing else there. Nobody was in the valley. I meditated in front of three white pagodas until the sun rose across smooth white stone and mud edge. The glare reflected in sunglasses intended to cut glare. I looked into the sunglasses inner edge, and realized my shadow was making a clockwise journey around me as I sat before the three pagodas. My shadow's journey would last only until the sun set on the other side of three pagodas. I remembered not to forget, that clocks cannot be turned backwards. The pagodas were pure white.

For Tibetans, white is the color of purity. For Han people, it is the color of death. For some reason white has been chosen as the color of pagodas which are often built upon the ashes of great Buddhist monks who spent their life seeking purity, in valleys which cannot be found because nobody remembers where they had walked before, or where the pagodas were built, until someone walks into the valley again, searching for them. If purity can only be buried under a white pagoda, then one can wait for death to become pure.

I began meditating on the color white.

My thoughts were interrupted by a nomad. He was wearing a dirty blanket riding on a horse. He laughed at me and asked where I was going. I explained that I was looking for Shangri-la. He offered me a ride.

I rode on the back of his horse, deeper into the valley. The valley had no roads, only a horse trail, formed in mud, by horse hooves. It was not a deliberate path. Nobody designed or approved it, or sought government funding or bank loans to build it. There were only horses passing this way sometimes frequently, sometimes not at all. There were also sheep and yak, sometimes herded by Tibetans riding horses. This is how the path came to be. It is a crossing remembered only by horses.

Deep in the valley we came upon black tents, woven of yak fur. These tents were the homes of nomads. We passed by a yak bull

which went insane. He was dragging tent poles on his back and being herded with the other yaks. He tore apart the tent on his back flinging poles everywhere. One might think that the bull had gone insane. On the other hand, he was just tired, of being herded with other yaks.

I left the nomads, and walked from here. I walked deeper into the valley. Deep in the valley I came upon a Tibetan woman, riding a snow white horse. She got off the horse and spoke to me. She was curious. I asked if I could ride the horse. She gave me the reigns and I got on. The horse threw me immediately. I pulled myself up off damp grass below two outstretched hands and shook my head. I had not been thrown by a horse since a kid. As a kid I had grown up riding horses. Perplexed I got back into the saddle. The horse ran. He ran like crazy. I realized that he did not intend to stop. I could not stop him. The saddle slipped to the side. The strap was not tight. Or maybe, I simply lost balance. Again I found myself on the ground, one foot caught in the stirrup. The horse dragged me for a few moments until I slipped my foot out. He continued to run ahead, in an uncertain direction. Eventually he stopped to chomp on grass.

The Tibetan lady ran over to me. She smiled as if nothing happened. "You ride him!" I said, shaking the dirt off of both hands angrily.

She smiled again. "He is a wild horse. I do not want to ride him either. He is very unpredictable," she said with innocence. If the horse was wild, then why did she let me ride it, I wondered. I looked into her eyes. Clearly she had not thought about this. If I wanted to ride a wild horse, then ride him.

She had a round face. On her head was a tall beige felt hat. Her hair was braided into thin tight braids favored by Tibetan women. "Such work takes at least four hours," she explained with pride. Turquoise and chunks of coral were braided into her hair. "These were my mother's," she touched them with feeling of connectivity to the past. "She gave these to me. I wear them every day." Grabbing the white horse by its leather reigns, she yanked him

84

from his grass munching. He followed reluctantly. "He is not a bad horse," she apologized, purity beaming from black Tibetan eyes. "He is not bad at all, not like other horses. He is just wild." I was beginning to understand the meaning of the color white.

She asked me where I was going. I said, "To Shangri-la." She shrugged her shoulders with indifference, and said almost as an afterthought, "I will take you. It is over there, in the next valley, this way." She led the way. We walked into the valley. Green rose to white capped mountains. Snow had taken refuge from summer there while freeing un-possessed ice tumbling into freezing rivers. Shadows of clouds crossed the valley and patterns of sunlight created an illusion of change as mountains stood still. In the distance an old lady sat before her yak fur tent. She held a baby, a grandchild. Into another generation, she was projecting spirit.

The Tibetan woman led her white horse pulling leather reigns, brought me further into the valley, above the river. She stopped where the horse neighed, before a black yak fur tent. We went inside where she introduced me to her friends, three women. One held a baby to her breast. It snuggled from cold, within layers of bright woven cloth, sucking milk. The tent was black, but not dark. Inside there was plenty of light. Within, one could see outside through pores of space between woven yak fur. While insulating against rain and cold, it provided light, almost transparency. The elements of space within filled with pungent smoke. A fire in the center of their tent exuded warmth. A pile of yak manure dried into hardened bricks beside the tent's entrance provided fuel for fire. Smoke drifted upward, mixing with a sharp blade of sunlight filtering into space from a hole directly above through which smoke escaped against crystal light into clear shrill blue air.

An eagle flew above. He was followed by more eagles. The women stepping from their tent pointed to the eagles and told me that there must be wolves below the eagles. Maybe a yak had died and would soon be consumed. One of the men came over with two boys. They had finished their morning work. Together they sat on blankets spread upon grass. The women sat beside them kneeling.

85

One boy played a Tibetan mandolin. It was the sound of three strings in a valley surrounded by snow capped mountains. We were the only ones in the valley with the sound of three strings. The man chanted. His voice called like an echo, rising as spirit, becoming thunder of wild horses running in uncertain directions. I listened in silence. He chanted. Together we watched the eagles.

## Yak Milk Cheese

A monk wandered across the river, into the valley. I did not know where he came from or when he joined us until I noticed he was there. Maybe I had not been looking carefully enough. Maybe it had something to do with the way Tibetan monks arrive. They don't arrive. They appear.

He appeared in saffron robes, head shaven, except for a small mustache and goatee. Smiling like an elf, he sat beside us and asked, "Where are you going?"

"I am searching for Shangri-la. Do you know where it is? What direction should I go in?"

His smile widened over his goatee stretching to pointed elf ears. With a flourish of his hand he offered to lead the way, into another valley narrower than the one we were in. A snow peak hovered over the crest of mountain above us. A freezing cold river ran before us. We followed the river, then, crossed it. Like an oasis in contrast, a tiny factory building stood before us across the river. We crossed upon the stones as there was no bridge. The stones had been rounded by freezing water. They were cold too. The Tibetan woman leading a white horse, followed.

The workers surprised by our sudden arrival stepped from the factory to greet us. Among them was a saffron robed monk, who introduced himself as head of the factory. I was to discover shortly he was head of an entire monastery as well.

"Factory?" I was shocked. "There is a factory here? What are you

87

factoring in the factory?"

"Cheese," explained the monk.

"Cheese?"

"Yes, cheese."

"How can you make cheese in a factory away from everything, everywhere, that is here?"

"We make yak milk cheese. We need to be near the yaks."

I thought for a moment as yak butter tea was poured before me by the Tibetan woman in a beige hat, whose white horse was now chomping grass. The monk running this factory was named Jigme Jensen. Within the next day or so he would not only change the way I think about cheese, but about business models and relationships between mountains, rivers, people, yak and education. I asked about yak milk cheese. He showed me his factory.

There were only three large rooms. But before we entered the rooms Jigme asked me to put on rubber boots and a white medics jacket, face mask, just as if I was entering an operating room. "We must keep international health standards here when making yak cheese for export," Jigme explained with a flourish of his hand as if he was about to wipe Dutch Gouda off the market. Sure enough, upon entering the factory, I could have stepped into a cheese factory outside Amsterdam. The same techniques were applied, yak milk churned in heated vats, settling into moulds, solidifying into cheese stored on wooden racks in cool rooms. I was convinced, Jigme Jensen was making cheese. Only one question remained. "Why here?"

"Because we need to be close to nomads who bring us fresh yak milk every morning and every evening through this door," Jigme pointed to a side door leading to the room with big hot churning vats.

"But you are nowhere near any point of distribution," I queried. There were no roads, point of connection. We were in the middle of nomad country in mountains within the heart of a "green sea".

"If you want to sell your cheese internationally, or even in China, you have to be manufacturing closer to infrastructure, distribution points," I volunteered the professional advice of a lawyer, business advisor.

"You see, I don't worry about distribution," Jigme was not interested in the urban advice I carried in my baggage. "I do not want to manufacture cheese in a place which might be inconvenient for nomads," he explained. "You see, I am manufacturing yak cheese."

It still didn't make sense. So what if you are making yak cheese in yak country. How to get the cheese to market? He still hadn't answered my question. "Excuse me, but it does not make any commercial sense to build a factory here just to provide convenience to nomads making yak milk deliveries."

"But that's just the point," Jigme insisted. "You see, they all live in mountains, in yak felt tents at high altitudes. They cannot leave the valleys so easily. So by having the factory here in mountains, they can deliver yak milk every day, even twice a day. In this way the milk is assured to be fresh."

I still did not understand this. "You can raise yak on farms near a factory near a city or point of distribution, right?"

"Wrong. It would not be wild yak milk," Jigme sighed, "that is milk from yaks herded by nomads. My real purpose is to help nomads."

Now I understood. Jigme Jensen explained that he had obtained investment from the Trace Foundation, established by Andrea Sorros' daughter of globalization financial guru of Asian financial crisis fame. Jigme used funds she donated to build the cheese factory in nomad country. The nomads traditionally had no income. Now without affecting their traditional life style, Jigme was providing income, by purchasing yak milk every day. In fact, he was not changing their traditional means of livelihood, but supporting it.

The hardship of distributing cheese from this isolated factory was Jigme's problem to overcome. Every day he would fill up a jeep with round cheese blocks and drive through mud and rivers out of mountains to the nearest cowboy town, then that long winding road to Xining, from which yak milk cheese would be exported to Europe, North America becoming the most exotic cocktail party contraption one could offer within chic wine tasting circles. Meanwhile, nomads had income, while keeping their traditional lifestyle intact. They continued to herd yak, live in yak tents, and ride wild white horses.

Jigme explained that since establishing the cheese factory, nomad income in the surrounding valleys and mountains had increased without affecting their life style. My question to Jigme was how to re-invest his own profits? Expand the cheese factory?

"No." Jigme explained that he had other ideas. He was about to build another school.

"Another school?"

"Yes, another school."

"Where? Here?"

"No. There." He pointed in a direction. "In the next valley, which is the valley after that next valley, below that other valley, yes the one over there. Do you understand? Yes, over there." Jigme pointed in an uncertain direction. "Would you like to see? I must go there tomorrow to determine the plot lines for walls of the school. After I determine which line should go in which direction, we will begin to build it with money from selling yak milk cheese to the world." I was beginning to understand Jigme's economic model for globalization of yak milk cheese. But I did not understand this

thing about a school.

The next morning we rose early to the sound of nomads delivering fresh yak milk to the factory's side door. The sound of pony hooves crushing dew dripping grassland had already evaporated from my mind as I rubbed my eyes. I stepped from the tent Jigme had pitched for me outside the factory, washing my face in the river below and wandering back. The nomads had left. "They come early to deliver yak's milk." Jigme explained. Afterwards, they return to the mountains.

Yak butter tea was poured into a bowl with *zamba* , a muesli looking wheat cereal. Jigme encouraged me to let yak butter tea absorb the *zamba*. Soon the yak butter tea had been absorbed by the cereal which became a pasty, sticky wheat pastry, something like a soft granola bar. I remembered when looking for Shangri-la in a cup of yak butter tea filled with *zampa*, to look carefully.

"This is *zampa*," explained Jigme. We Tibetans eat it breakfast, lunch and sometimes for dinner. *Zampa* is the basic staple at all Tibetan meals."

"You know, this tastes like muesli, a western style cereal. I think you could export this with the cheese," I suggested. "It would go over real well with all the new age health types, and in organic food stores. That's a great name too, highly marketable with that crowd. It would be a hit in California. Just call it *zampa*."

"I have already registered the '*Zampa*' trademark," Jigme nodded.

With a flourish of his saffron robe, Jigme led me into his jeep driven by another monk. Jigme sat in front, and I sat squeezed in between two other monks in back. I was the only one not wearing saffron. We bounced down the narrow trail driving through rivers, balancing across collapsing ridges. Eventually we followed a river into a valley, then into another valley. Jigme pointed excitedly out the window. "See that tent in the distance. There are two young children in that nomad family, girls. Do you see that tent there," he pointed in another direction. I could barely see a tent on the horizon surrounded by tiny dots, yak. "There are several more girls living there. None of them has any opportunity to go to school because they are nomads, living here in mountains. I will bring the

92

school to them. They will be my students."

We drove into another valley, and sure enough several workers were there painting wall lines of what would be a school on rounding, flattening portion of grassland. Jigme jumped out of the jeep and strode over to them, arguing over where the lines should be drawn to make more room for the classrooms, more like a construction site boss than a monk. The line was adjusted. The classroom would be a bit bigger.

Rising above the valley was a sharp mountain, its surface cliff. Jigme broke his attention away from questions of building foundation to point at the cliff. Small dots could be seen at a point two thirds up to the top. "There are caves there," he whispered. "Monks used to come to this place for meditation. It is a good location for a school."

Still I was perplexed. "But why don't you build the school closer to town? The children can go there and stay in a dorm. Return to their parents on holiday. It would be so much easier."

"You see, their parents all live in the mountains, in yak felt tents at high altitudes. They cannot leave the valleys so easily. So by having the school here in mountains, they can go to school every day, and then go home to be with their parents twice a day. Their traditional life style will not be affected. I do not want to build a school in a place which might be inconvenient for nomads."

"What will the school be like?"

Jigme waved me back into the jeep. We drove up the hill, along a ridge crest, following a path without any road. The driver was following his instincts. The entrance to this valley would lead to a river which would lead out from another valley. Within a matter of hours we had left the mountains. We arrived back to the cowboy town I had crashed in just a day or two before. It somehow seemed like a long time ago as if time had been lost in valleys and mountains.

We drove through the cowboy town. Tibetan cowboys in big hats driving motorcycles were still driving back and forth as if it was the same movie I had watched several days ago except that John Wayne was not because the Muslims kept a monopoly on lamb shank and the Navahos had become Tibetans. Woosh...the doors of a small restaurant spun open as a Tibetan in sharp cowboy boots, tall hat and big plastic sunglasses pushed his way into the street standing off sharply in front of another Tibetan. He gave him a tough look in the eye, then swinging unto his heavy metal motorcycle, drove off into the sunset, leaving only a stream of dust settling behind.

Jigme was oblivious to all this and signaled to his driver who sped through the little town toward a gate which was opened by other monks. We entered. Before me was a Tibetan style building beautifully constructed of stone and wood with fresh bright paintings of colorful horses, monkeys and elephants. A monk unlocked the clean glass doors and nodded in deference as Jigme explained that it was summer break, so all the students had gone home to their parents. He invited me in.

On the first floor, Jigme led me into a physics lab full of modern equipment, then into a chemistry lab. I followed him down the hallway, colorful Tibetan paintings on the walls, into a small library. It was filled with books both Chinese and Tibetan. There were copies of sacred text written on traditional long Tibetan paper in a cabinet. There were also copies of American books, even Disney cartoons for kids. "Tibetan children like Mickey Mouse," Jigme noted as he led me upstairs.

On the second, top floor of this little school we entered classrooms filled with computers, the latest internet equipment, Qinghai on line. Jigme then turned on a computer and showed me how the written Tibetan language is now digitized, used for internet communication throughout the greater Qinghai-Tibetan plateau. Jigme explained that his school was offering nomad children 24 hour global internet access for free. "They can come in to these rooms after school and go on line. We encourage that. They can be connected to the world from our little school in Qinghai."

Jigme Jensen went on to explain, "It is the first private school in this region, meaning we have had no government funding support. So we did it on our own. Our school welcomes any nomad children to attend regardless of ethnicity or religion. We have both Tibetans, Muslims and Manchurians. At our school education is free. It is all paid for with cheese."

94

# Meditation

As we left the school Jigme and I walked along the Yellow River, brown, gold, glistening across its flat surface in the morning sun against banks of red soil washed flat by the river known throughout history as "China's Sorrow". "Yes, this is the Yellow River, the mother river of all Chinese," Jigme said. "The Yellow River's origin is here, Ma Duo County. Travel along the river. After two large bends in the river, from this spot, you will come to its origin. According to the landscape of Buddhism, this curve in the river before our monastery is a very good place. So our ancestors chose to build Lajia Temple situated here, because this is the best place." He led me to the place.

Inside Lajia monastery is a temple. We entered the temple. Past rows of candles we passed, I followed Jigme Jensen. Candles led through darkness, which became light when he held aloft a tiny brass cup of yak butter oil, a burning light flickered, eating oil on the surface of yak butter. Rows of candles on all sides of this temple barely illuminated Thankas and statutes of Buddha, teachers, bodhisattvas and guardians. Flames floated delicately upon clear surface of yak butter carefully placed in each brass cup by monks in the early morning before reciting mantra. They flicker gently as we walk past, response to the presence of two people, passing a flame without noticing its presence.

"Now we say this whole Qinghai-Tibetan plateau is Shangri-la," Jigme Jensen explained, "but Shangri-la is not only one spot. The city where Mi Le Buddha stays is called Shangri-la, it is also Xiang

95

Ba, which means 'kind mother'. The people who are doing good things can find Shangri-la. Shangri-la refers to you reaching the level where the Buddha reaches."

Jigme then led me up a path behind the temple. The path rose to a point within the shadow of sharp cliffs reaching upward to clear blue above, touched only by the passing of white clouds which soon dispersed. "The 9th Panchen Lama came here and stayed in this temple," Jigme explained. "There is a Panchen Palace on the hillside above this temple." He pointed to the palace, now decaying adobe. "It is a place cultivated by a Lama," clearly a good place. The Lama had long left. The place untouched had presence.

"The whole Qinghai-Tibetan Plateau can be called Shangri-la," Jigme said. "People here are closer to Buddhism, since their birth. Therefore, their hearts are more kind. Compare with some polluted big cities, the place without pollution can be called Shangri-la, but it is not real Shangri-la. I have these poor students, and give to them the opportunity to study. It can be said that I am doing a good thing, something which other people should also do. The most basic way to find Shangri-la is you yourself must have a good heart,

and give to others." Jigme went on to explain, "According to your route, you have already found many Shangri-la. But to find the real Shangri-la, you must do things from your heart. Through doing good things for others you can find the real Shangri-la."

A dry dusty path weaves between buildings made of mud, brick, adobe, casabas of compartments in the beehive of Lajia monastery. Monks in saffron robes walk past, oblivious to dust. It whirls in concentric circles and settles where nobody bothers to look. "But why was the Lajia Temple built here?" I asked. Is it because of a bend in the Yellow River near but still not yet at the source of the river? Why did the 9th Panchen Lama choose to come to this isolated place, to stay in the Lajia Temple? Why had Jigme Jensen become a bodhisattva in disguise, bringing education to children of nomads who had been forgotten by the rest of the world? I was curious, and asked Jigme to tell me more.

He said nothing, but brought me to a hillside above Lajia Temple, beside altars where pine branches burned as incense, the final point before sheer cliffs which rise above the monastery. Energy emanates from the cliffs. Below aeries of white eagles, there are

caves in the cliffs. Monks have come to these caves to meditate for centuries, some still come today. Once, over 40 monks meditated in these caves at the same time, creating compact space of concentration between the realm of eagles and the flow of a long winding river reflecting clouds passing in the sky. Jigme told me to sit on this spot, beside altars of pine incense, cross legged for a prolonged period of time. He asked me to meditate.

Meditation concentrates concentration. It can bring one to their most central point of being, oneself without self. It is a process of arrival and departure without leaving or asking too specifically where you have just come from or where you will go next.

Concentration is focused on mantra, prayer of giving and death, a call to white eagles encircling above. Acutely aware of all which passes below, they too can hear mantra uttered in the most elemental realm of your own subconscious.

Pine incense is lost in wind between cliffs, where 40 monks once meditated in silence, but have now gone their own way. If you think that you have heard their breathing in the wind, it is only an illusion. In fact they are long gone. Their flesh has already been eaten by white eagles. They too have flown to lost aeries only to die and be forgotten. Their feathers have dispersed in the wind. So all you can hear is the sound of your own meditation. It is the silence of concentration between deep breaths.

# Sound of Snow Melting

They pray to sun,
fire necessity
life philosophy.
If your dream is fire,
you can understand
the rationale
of burning mist.

Misty valleys,
cold rivers rush,
along ancient stone alleys
villages soon forgotten
only remembered
by water sound
in an empty
cup of tea.

Before snow mountains
stop, wait, listen
to melting snow sounds
echo children chanting,
call from wilderness
is a purple moon,
crying in the rain.

# YUNNAN

# Alternative Space

Kunming on a rainy morning, rain trickles in grey shadows along tree lined streets. The old Kunming of two story natural wood and grey tile shop houses and homes I remembered from years ago was gone. On all sides around me, concrete slabs with blue glass stretched to the sky. Aside from old trees, there was nothing of old Kunming left. I saw my shadow of twenty years ago, a student with backpack, wandering among old buildings, buying French baguettes and black coffee of yesterday's Kunming. My memories vanished as black rain turned to grayish mist.

I followed an address given to me by my friend Cheng Xingdong, who divides his time between Beijing and Paris representing artists. Xingdong believed in the expressive power of China's upcoming artists. He saw in art circles of Beijing the emergence of salons as in Paris during another era, fusion of creative people's collective imagination giving birth to an entire milieu of art. He could see this happening because he had the perspective of someone born in China who had lived for a long time in Paris. It was this historic glance which gave him perspective. So he had brought the artists together one after another in exhibitions in his old courtyard home in Beijing, inviting ambassadors and businessmen, a Paris art salon in old Beijing, a platform for bringing their art to Paris, to the international stage. But he too was afraid developers might tear down his courtyard home to make way for more cement and blue glass. Meanwhile, Beijing's artists had all fled to Kunming. There was no inspiration for them left in Beijing, only cement and traffic. They were all going southwest, as far from the center as possible. They were trying to escape the cement and traffic. Maybe they were searching for Shangri-la. Maybe they were all just fed up.

"Yunnan has become China's center of alternative culture. Artists and intellectuals are now gathering there. It is a focal point of new ideas and creativity," Xingdong had explained to me back in Beijing. The momentum of such a movement had to be put into context he noted. "The history of Yunnan is fusion. From our point of view, Yunnan was historically borderland, where troops banned people, prisoners. Han culture had to cross mountains to get there, so due to its isolation, pure culture of ethnic minority tribes has persisted there. Because of Yunnan's multi-ethnicity, people there have a more open way of thinking, unlike Beijing and Shanghai. Beijing was the ancient capital, the emperor's political epicenter, so a mainstream culture emanates from there. Shanghai has historically been China's open port to the west, so western ideas come into Shanghai easily, but these are all of a commercial nature which is what drives the place. Yunnan is different."

Xingdong encouraged me to go to Yunnan. I first visited the province in the early 1980s when it was a backwater, not an easy place to trek through. I had not been back for a decade. Now it was the happening art scene. "It is where people go to get away from the mainstream, from commerce." Xingdong suggested I meet some artist friends there living in converted warehouses. "By the very nature of its environment, its isolation and multi-ethnicity, it is

the borderland," he explained scratching a few addresses and mobile phone numbers of artists on a piece of paper. He handed me the paper. "This is where you go to find the alternative."

I found the alternative in an alleyway behind a set of factory warehouses at an address given to me by Xingdong. These factory warehouses had been turned into art galleries and studios. Beside studios and in between alleyways which split off from other main alleyways, in places wide enough for stray cats to jump headlong down from a drainage pipe into an open trash can and to make the jump like an acrobat without spilling trash laterally across the tiny existing space between broken brick walls, tiny cafes and wine bars had opened, a subterfuge oasis for artists in need of an afternoon caffeine injection or a non-hallucinatory wind-down between excessive paint inhalation from abstract expression of one's inner emotions or external frustrations. I got off a public bus and found the alleyway. In the alleyway I found an artist, Ye Yongqing sipping a double café latte with a look of contemplation on his face as if he were anticipating from which direction the stray cat above would jump in order to not miss the soft cushion of garbage in an open trash can. I sat with him and joined the process of contemplating a stray cat's late afternoon acrobatics, a lesson in balance.

The space we sat in was actually a narrow alley with factory warehouses on each side. The factories had collapsed and gone bust because they were run according to state plans which did not fit in with the new market economy. Ye Yongqing had found it when he got sick of all the noise and bulldozing in Beijing, coming to Yunnan in search of quiet chunks of space to sit in and paint. Then other artists came. They rented the collapsing warehouses from the factories. They renovated them, turning these cavernous rooms into studios. Then hip restaurateurs came to open chic eateries, wine bars and cafes. Every night the factory warehouses and alleyways between buzzed with life, laughter and new ideas until sunrise. By noontime the artists were waking up again, painting and receiving foreign agents and dealers. The most run-down factory neighborhood space had become transformed into the hottest, most expensive second-hand rental commercial real estate in town under the noses of state owned enterprise managers who could still not figure out what was happening with their bankrupt factory

104

warehouses. As I sat in the espresso alleyway chatting with Ye, I noticed some photos framed on a brick wall behind him. "Where are those photos from?" I asked.

"They are from an artist who lives in Beijing," Ye explained. "He divides his time between Beijing and Dali, and has a special interest in local children there. These are his newest photos, countryside children. They may lack material possessions of city kids, but inside they are very happy. Look at their faces. You can tell."

"What they lack in material things, they make up in spiritual."

"He also did some TV stuff at the same time, those small children were very curious about this kind of modern media equipment. The teachers all told them, they must not touch it, very expensive equipment that their family could not afford to buy if broken, even if they spent their whole life working to do so. But these kids are very happy. So you have to ask yourself why so many artists are now coming to Dali from Beijing to set up work studios. They discovered you still can enjoy life doing things they like without having to spend all their time thinking and talking about making money.

"Is that the reason why so many artists are coming to Yunnan, what is the real reason?"

"In the present environment, artists have changed into nomads, they move around various cultures. They can live in different cultures and experiment with different ideas simultaneously. In this free state of mind, they are searching for a life style which will fit them. There are many European artists who find themselves in a similar situation. For example, there are some artists who might live in Germany will also have a studio in Italy or Paris, to divide a part of their life. This kind of geographic nomadic behavior brings a broader perspective over one culture. This tells us that when human being searches for his soul, he must walk a very long road. It is like you now walking on this road, searching for Shangri-la."

He then took a sip from his coffee cup, and thought about what he was saying. He thought for a moment longer than one might expect,

but it seemed like seconds before he lifted up his head. I wondered if he had found Shangri-la in his cup of café latte. He seemed to be looking carefully enough. "Actually to me, searching for Shangri-la is like searching for a road home. We do not need to prove what Hilton described in his book. People are constantly trying to find Hilton's Shangri-la excavated in a piece of wood or a piece of grass. Shangri-la can be excavated around everybody. This generation of ours over the past 20 years have constantly sought a free open environment, which in turn has brought us into contact with a variety of different cultures. Cultural integration is an open process. Meanwhile, we look back to our Chinese tradition. Regardless of whether you are looking back to your own tradition or integrating other cultures is not the point. The purpose is go back to your own daily life, ask how to live your everyday life, go back to find everybody's real life. Why have different artists from different places come to Kunming? They are coming for one reason alone, to open up their minds and to change their everyday life."

"It seems to me that you are not only providing an environment here for painting and creating, but also for incorporating art work into life, into an alternative or maybe more real life style?" I asked,

"Is that what's happening?"

"Correct, this is the most important and most basic thing taking place here. I have also seen many similar kinds of places. Artists always remain at a distance from society. We call this alternative life, the idea of living at the fringe of society. The things artists want to do are always pushed aside by mainstream society, so artists hang themselves in the air, and in turn cannot land down. So how do we let them land on the ground? Artists should set themselves against the public. So this environment here is not like a western functioning gallery or a pure art center, which operates on a set of business principles, a model. It in fact is neither, but can be either. It is an unstable system, but this unstable system may be more active and alive, holding out a variety of possibilities, real life styles, easier to approach. It is real."

I thought about what Ye was saying. It was true. Western art galleries operate on the basis of an economic model: artist, agent, gallery, collector, all integrated into a fixed system of mainstream recognition driven by commercially driven media. Room for the alternative does not really exist outside of defined boundaries of what should be alternative, meaning that what is chic is in fact mainstream. Alternative writers and artists are destined to sit between trash cans in a city street and beg to support their creativity as the mainstream determines what should be creative and what should not. In fact, in mainstream society, those who determine recognized art, have no creativity. It's purely business.

"Western art galleries have a system," explained Ye. "This system does not exist in China. All third world countries lack it. I have traveled through many different countries over the past few years, and frankly found the third world art scene much more exciting than what was happening in Europe or the US. I felt more close to them. These countries have no art galleries, no so called 'contemporary art professional system'. Art to those people means what? I have been considering this question a lot. In their life, what are the methods people use to approach art. They in fact live in what we call alternative space, and this alternative space has provided a new model. It combines traditional and modern, professional and folk, merged together with some outstanding intellectual ideas. These things they produce are full of creative energy, because they actually relate to what we are discussing, a spiritually not materially driven force."

"So could we say that it is a quest for the spiritual in escaping the material which has led so many of the art circles here in searching for Shangri-la?"

"It is certain that some of artists came here because of interest in Tibetan culture. All artists have some Tibetan culture in their hearts. Not long ago, a Hong Kong magazine 'Ming Bao' undertook an investigative search for Shangri-la. The journalists started from Kunming, went to Dali, then Lijiang, Jianchuan, Zhongdian, then eventually arrived in Nujiang. This road leading to the Tibetan area, we call 'the road of art ecology'. There are many artists scattered on this road. They are from Beijing, Guangzhou, even Taiwan, some American artists or Japanese artists went there as well. The ones who have money will buy a house, those who do not, will rent a place. They run bars and just live there. There are also people like us, migratory birds, we do not buy a house, but come here every year, to get together with these people, to feel mountains, rivers, sky, the earth, to hike, to enjoy different scenery."

"So then this must be the road to Shangri-la, right?"

"It is neither right nor wrong. Everybody is searching for Shangri-la in their own way. It is not important for us in fact. You do not have to look for it purposely. However it is related to these landforms, and is related to this route. All these routes to me means friends, there are people who love their life. Of course, there are mountains, rivers, sky and earth which move you too. The most important are human feelings, history, and your memories of it. Kunming is my hometown, but like all cities in China, changing very fast. All modern cities in China have been changed so that they have no history, no character, no tradition, faceless without meaningful lifestyle, all changed to be the same. How can this kind of city keep people, keep memories without human feeling. We, ordinary people, have lost the things we loved, but we were not able to change it. We can only go back to our small environment to create a homeland of our own, add our love to it. Like those artists we just visited in the lofts upstairs, they are building and

108

creating their own life. Living inside, they find and bring back a so-called Shangri-la, bit by bit."

"So then there is no road to Shangri-la?"

Ye Yongqing thought for a moment as he stared into his empty cup of café latte, as if he was searching for something which maybe was not there. He stared. The cup was empty. I knew he was searching carefully. "Artists devote all their lives to create different work, but work is not purpose, this work is also the artist in search of his own life's process, it is also a part of his life," he explained. "Without this kind of life, he cannot create this kind of work, without creating this kind of work, he will not dream for this kind of life. Searching for Shangri-la is a process. You are always in the process of searching for it."

When I left the alleyway tucked between warehouses which had become the space of artists, in the process of seeking something which could be called Shangri-la if you searched for it long enough in a cup of café latte, I noticed an old broken sofa on top of one of the buildings. As I began to hitchhike down the road I thought about the lonely sofa on top of a broken warehouse which had now become the most expensive real estate in Kunming because artists were turning around disregarded space into a realm of creative energy.

I thought about the energy, then thought about that sofa and wondered to myself which artist might occupy it each day, sitting on it to reflect between painting sessions, feeling between the rip in torn blue jeans pain of sharp decrepit springs piercing through a ragged sofa cover, while staring at pigeons flying above between lofts of warehouses, which could be white eagles on a vast Tibetan plain, if one closed their eyes long enough to reflect within the black sensation created by pretending to turn off all the lights of a warehouse studio loft to walk around blindfolded without any clothes on for a time frame limited to five minutes so you don't knock over the paints or easel. In moments like this one can arrive at a specific point of clarity. It is sometimes called, alternative space.

# No One Listens

I hitchhiked down the road, outside Kunming. New highways were being built over what was once red clay earth. I thought that new highways would be very convenient for motorists in the future. Certainly there would be a lot more cars in Kunming in the future. I thought how convenient it would be. And then thought how I would miss the red clay under my feet.

Yunnan means "south of the clouds". Beneath the clouds is red clay which ethnic minorities of Yunnan have carved with their hands across millennium into rice and coffee terraces. If you flew in a low plane or took enough hallucinations to believe that you were flying somewhere between the clouds and clay, you could see in this spectrum of sun and rain which in convergence is south, the level plateaus, terraces carved by hand, by those who still care for clay. In the sunlight, after rain, they become a spectrum of color. This is caused by the contraction of sunlight touching a thin water surface which rests between banks of soft dirt and red clay beneath.

As the truck dumped me off I walked across a tread-run dirt road and found myself standing before high clay walls. This was the address which Xingdong in Beijing had given me. He said I would come to a place which was not really a place because it could only be identified by high clay walls. When I found these walls, I would find Luo Xu's studio. Luo Xu had spent his entire life working with clay. He had done so as artist, and before that as construction worker. In the Cultural Revolution he had to dig mud. So when I found high walls which were not made of cement covered with

bathroom tiles and blue glass of every single construction site in China, but rather a wall made of just soft, reddish, brownish, yellowish hardened clay, I knew that I had come to the right place, Luo Xu's studio.

I found Luo Xu living behind the high walls surrounding his studio. The studio was also his home. Behind the walls was a beat-up 1950s era car, the type used by Stalin or other communist leaders, covered with a hallucination of spray paint colors. Inside the compound was a garden, with wild flowers growing uncontained.

Vast seemingly beehive structures dominated the garden. Each was constructed of clay bricks. I was to discover that these were catacomb structures built by Luo Xu to permanently display his art. In each catacomb stood towering figures, legs of women interwoven creating huge terrifying insect images, clay torsos and bodies in positions of pleasure and pain. And everywhere one could see Luo Xu's trademark heads, ceramic extended necks with heads, mouths open laughing, screaming and crying. The heads were stacked together like crowds in a city, going to work, jammed on a lunch break, leaving work, but never leaving the city.

111

I had seen all the museums in New York, Paris, London, Amsterdam, Barcelona, but never had I seen such a creative, ingenious museum as the huge beehive catacombs single handedly constructed out of brick from his own kiln by Luo Xu. But this was not an art gallery, not a museum. People were not invited to come to see Luo Xu's art. In fact, he did not want to be bothered by people at all. He was purposely displaying art, for nobody to see at all.

"How long ago did you move here to establish your studio?" I asked.

"Yes, about 6 to 7 years ago," he thought for a moment, sitting cross legged on a Chinese stool. He poured some tea and lit another cigarette which puts one in the mood to think. After thinking some more he added almost as an afterthought, "I came here in 1995."

"I can see that not many people visit your place now," I said out loud without thinking. Only a lone donkey Luo Xu kept as his "friend" stood in the garden. The donkey had full reign over Luo Xu's space. He would eat some wild flowers, walk among the talking or screaming heads, and sometimes nudge Luo Xu who affectionately pet the donkey's short fur on the flat area between its eyes. "Maybe you do not like them to visit here," I thought more clearly. "Is that correct?"

"I am not very social person. I cannot be calm with too many annoying people around. However, if someone can bring something of interest to me, I can sacrifice a bit of time. The problem is that people normally bring nothing to me except noise. I have no interest in noise."

"A lot of people are trying to escape noise nowadays. Many Beijing artists are coming to Yunnan, seeking a quite, calm environment away from big busy city life," I took a sip of tea. The donkey nudged his nose into my cup.

"In our history Yunnan was lost in high mountains, far away from the emperor," Luo Xu explained. "So for thousands of years the emperor really did not know what was happening in Yunnan. The court in Beijing only knew there was a place called Yunnan which

112

was a part of the empire. For centuries it was isolated, depending entirely on itself. In old days, the emperor banned those Chinese he did not like to Yunnan because it was considered wilderness, a distant outpost, the last place to be banished. Many of the ethnic Chinese here today are descendants of those left over from then. At that time there were only ethnic minorities in Yunnan, each with their own small kingdoms, lots of what we call in Chinese tu huangdi local emperors, basically warlords. To a great extent the psychological framework of this time persists today. There is big difference between Yunnan and the rest of China." In these words, Luo Xu explained why so many artists were congregating in Yunnan, each in a way banished by the mainstream, seeking distance from the center, escaping all the noise.

The donkey began wandering toward at an old Yunnan style courtyard home which had been re-assembled and restored on one corner of the property. "Luo Xu, is that your old house?" I asked pointing at the courtyard.

"Yes. When my home town started what they call 'city construction', they wanted to destroy it. I brought it here and restored it. Now the entire old town is destroyed, everything torn down. At that time I felt terrible. I did not have the means or capital to save more. I really wanted to keep them all. Move them to another place to keep them. There were many very grand old houses. This one was just an ordinary one."

"Of the entire ancient town, at least you were able to save this one home, while developers were busy destroying the rest. This is happening all over China," I pointed out. "Look at Beijing. They have literally obliterated the city's heritage."

"I think Chinese people are very interesting," Luo Xu sighed, drinking his tea, one eye thoughtfully watching his donkey chewing wild flowers, moving gradually closer to his old restored home. "A powerful energy lies, hiding within them," Luo explained. "If there is a direction, everybody will follow. The situation is like when Chairman Mao waved his hand, everybody would start to destroy things, even start to criticize their own parents. This aspect of

113

Chinese people's energy is quite unique. Maybe many years later, the next generation or the generation after the next generation, there will be an explosion of energy among the young people who will tear down all the architecture of the 1980s and 1990s. This energy is a very interesting characteristic of Chinese people. Look at the classic architecture of old Beijing and even Kunming. In their eyes this old architecture is poor and backwards. One day, when the future generation sees what we have now, they may dismantle all these houses too. It is quite possible. China's several thousands of years of mass movements have witnessed this kind of terrible thing, especially in modern times. Today you have tired people and wasted money. They only know how to dismantle one thing and put up another thing. They do not know how to use it, protect it, and feel for it. In my mind the past architecture and culture are like my parents. Think of an old man. No matter how senile this old man may be, he is your parent. The old house is the same. Despite the lack of modern conveniences, it is still your parent. You cannot kick out your parents because they are old. Nowadays, people tear down old houses just like kicking out their old parents, thinking they are old, ugly, a burden. In fact, an old man sitting there quietly, does not disturb anybody. He is just sitting there happily and quietly, he didn't disturb you, moreover he brought you up."

Luo Xu pointed out that Chinese culture always promoted respect for elderly people, taking care of small children, respecting parents. In turn, he could not understand the rapid and accelerating erosion of such values over recent years. Maybe it was caused by the wild rush to become western. Maybe it was caused by newfound love of money and all the things it can buy. "You dislike and look down upon these old houses," he said of developers and some officials alike. "You want to decorate yourself like a European rich family, not a Chinese farmer. A farmer, an old man, old houses have natural self-grown flowers, self-grown grass, free flying birds in the sky, animals in the woods. The roots of all these things are the same. They are living together. In fact they are very comfortable. Now some cultural and economic phenomena violates the basic rule that many things must live together to survive in this world, which makes the world interesting. Now the new rule is to only allow one thing

114

to exist. But only seeking one thing is too simple. China for the past few years has crazily used porcelain tiles, smothering all new concrete buildings with these tiles. This is a big joke. The demand for porcelain tiles in China must be the greatest in the world."

Luo Xu was referring to the phenomena of old historic buildings being torn down by developers, only to be replaced by cement blobs covered with bathroom tiles. Such structures now were standard. You can drive through almost any city or town in China and see them everywhere, one building after another, all the same, covered with bathroom tiles and blue glass. "In foreigners' eyes, these kind of white porcelain tiles are used to decorate toilets," I pointed out. Yes, it seemed to many foreigner observers that China's urban planners while obliterating their nation's architectural heritage, had in Freudian terms an infatuation with designing building exteriors to look like public rest room interiors. "This kind of thing

represents the current mood in China, blindly copying western things without understanding what they are all about."

"China is trying its best to learn from the west. Hong Kong has learned from the west. So China thinks Hong Kong is the closest to the west, so they learn everything from Hong Kong. I have thought about this thing, as with anything, first you have to have a feeling about it, be familiar with it. It is like a bird building its little house. It is built very scientifically because a bird is very familiar with a piece of rattan, how to use sticky dirt. The reason is it deals with these elements everyday. So we can see a birdhouse is done casually and elegantly, because it is so familiar with the elements it uses. Unfamiliar means it has no feeling for something, so it can only blindly admire it. The unfamiliar image will not fit you. Western people have been using steel and cement for many years. It took so many years in Europe to create modern architecture in the context of their history and cultural changes. They are very familiar with these elements of theirs. They have feeling for it. Do Chinese people have such feeling? Over the course of thousands of years of Chinese history, we Chinese people have slept with wood and bricks. Ask yourself, how come we have the Forbidden City? There is no Forbidden City in Europe. Likewise, there are no good modern cities in China." Luo Xu leaned over. His donkey was strolling back for more attention. He began petting the donkey on its forehead between its eyes. Its ears perked. "Any animal knows itself why it needs to grow a certain color of fur. There is a reason for him to grow such fur. Because it has gone through several thousand years of evolution, it looks like this. It is just as if I suddenly changed the color of my skin. I will still not be like white people. A flower is a flower, a tiger is a tiger."

Luo Xu then asked me why I had come to Yunnan to hang with artists. I explained that I had started my trip in Lhasa hanging with monks, traveling through Qinghai hanging with nomads. He understood, nodded, and lit another cigarette. I explained that "Not only Chinese artists but a lot of foreigners are getting fed up with the fatigue of urban values. They too are escaping to quiet places in western China, searching for Shangri-la."

116

"This is a current direction, a trend. However," he sipped tea petting his donkey. "I think differently. Actually, a quiet place can be found anywhere. I think quiet places can be found in cities too. Of course, this requires seeking energy within oneself." Luo Xu observed three kinds of Shangri-la seekers. "There are many big-shot city artists, who buy houses to rest here and then go back to the city. They have not actually moved to this place, they do not really feel the earth here. However on the surface they find this place to be very quiet. This kind of person is only escaping reality. Another kind of person is really fed up with city life from the bottom of their heart. They want to completely change their working and living style. In the process of doing so, they eventually found it impossible to leave this place. The third kind of person has no idea of what this place should look like; they do not know why they stayed in the city in the first place. They saw other people coming here, so they followed too."

I thought about what Luo Xu was saying. Yes, Yunnan's ancient towns of Dali and Lijiang had become not just artist colonies but backpacker paradises as well. Both Lijiang and Zhongdian County had been embroiled in conflict over which place was the original Shangri-la described in Hilton's novel "Lost Horizon". "Should I go to Lijiang, or Zhongdian County?" I asked Luo Xu. "Some people say that the real Shangri-la is there. What do you think?"

"Many places claim themselves as Shangri-la. Lijiang, Zhongdian, Tibet, Qinghai, even towns in Sichuan are competing with each other for this name. Sure, these areas all have a connection to Tibetan Buddhism. But the sad irony is they are competing for this name entirely for commercial objectives, without understanding the concept of what Shangri-la is really all about. In fact, you can find Shangri-la everywhere in the Qinghai-Tibetan plateau, in every blade of grass. It is not a place which can be designated by any single person. I think Shangri-la is a concept, very natural, peaceful like heaven, a realm of self survival, vital energy, very wild and elemental. But this does not mean it can be found in any particular place. To actually find it would be too disappointing. If the author who wrote 'Lost Horizon' woke up now, he would not tell us that it was ever his intention to find where

117

Shangri-la is really located."

"Then am I taking the correct road to Shangri-la?"

"Most people do not dare go to these places because they are afraid of high altitude sickness. Europeans who came here did not feel comfortable, even Chinese people do not, even in their own country. In fact, Chinese people's life is getting better now, so they are especially afraid of getting sick. They are afraid that they will step on something and fall down, so they are afraid of the possible and most don't dare go of to Zhongdian. In having a better life, they are now afraid of losing what they have. Actually, you should go there. Reaction to high altitude is nothing, maybe a bit difficult to breath, but not as serious as people say." Unfortunately, it seemed materialism had become the overriding value of China. While the material west was seeking something spiritual in the east, China had already lost what it had to give. Chinese would not go to Shangri-la for fear that it might cost them their materialism, both literally and spiritually. Pondering this thought, left me shocked, feeling quite empty inside, disappointed.

"You are from Yunnan originally. When did you first go to Zhongdian?" I was really curious when Luo Xu himself first explored Shangri-la.

"My first time to Zhongdian was five years ago, late summer same season as now. One moment it rained. Another it cleared. When I arrived there was a glimmer of sunlight scattered on top of some small distant hills. Because of rain, it was not very clear, creating a pattern of strange colors in the sky, hard to describe. If Lamas saw this, they would think such colors as a gift from heaven, lie down, prostrate themselves and meditate. They respect pure natural beauty very much, and express their feelings toward nature with the totality of their emotions. They might stand there nervously, shaking with emotion, even write poems on the spot. I think at such moments, one's eyes are no use as communication with nature is already coming directly from one's heart communicating. In such situations, don't bother taking photos. You take a photo, go back and look at it. Then it has no meaning anymore.

Why? In such moments a human being merges with nature. At that very moment, I melted, disappeared, and was digested into that place. This was my first trip to Zhongdian."

"The question then is not where, but what is Shangri-la?

"As for finding Shangri-la, I think Zhongdian should be the right place, because it has not been torn up by human beings yet. Such a mysterious concept as Shangri-la cannot lie in a city. At the same time we cannot use our finger to point at any single place and say it is Shangri-la; we can only use our heart to tell us what Shangri-la is. Shangri-la can be found. It lies inside your heart. Everyone can look within themselves, and find their own Shangri-la."

Luo Xu then led me into one of the beehive catacomb buildings exhibiting his work. The cavernous brick room was round, like an auditorium. On one side were rows and rows of the heads which he sculpted from ceramic. Some were laughing, some crying, others screaming, or so it seemed to me. The figures all faced him in rows one tier upon another, in a half circle, like singers in a choir. "Do you know what I like to do more than anything else in the world?" Luo Xu asked me with a look on his face of forlorn sincerity, or unrepentant intention.

"What?" I asked with curiosity.

Luo Xu pointed to the heads facing us. He then pointed to a CD player in the corner. "I like to play music very loud in this room, classic music. I then stand in the center before all of these heads I have created, and conduct. I can do this for hours."

On any given day, at an undetermined time, Luo Xu will stand before the heads he had created, exploding with expression, some laughing, some crying, others screaming. Luo Xu will then put the music up loudly, and wave his hands slowly, like a conductor before a choir. He will conduct for hours. But the heads will remain silent. On such occasions, his pet donkey will sit there attentively, and listen. Aside from the donkey, no one listens.

# Purple Moon Crying in Rain

Kunming. The old city is now gone. Wood, stone and tile houses have been smashed, obliterated and covered with cement. For some it is economic progress, for others, the uprooting of their roots. I followed an address San Bao gave me, to a non-descript building. I cannot remember it could have been a factory which seemed to

have been converted into a school. I was to discover it was a half built theatre. I stood outside looking at cement walls and smudged glass windows. It was raining in the parking lot.

I heard the sound of chanting. It rang through my ears with a piercing sound like a call from wilderness, the cry of a purple moon in rain. It haunted the recesses of my thoughts. The echo reverberated for a time which could not be measured by the sound of breath. I followed the sound up four flights of cement stairs and entered a dance studio. The children stood on both sides, their tiny bodies draped in traditional clothing of their village. It had been sewn three generations ago, passed from grandmother, to mother, to daughter. They were proud of their clothes. They were unaware of my presence. They were singing.

I found Yang Liping, China's legendary dance performer, sitting on the floor against a mirror wall of her studio, back pressed against the mirror. Village girls singing were reflected in the mirror, in the sun glasses of Yang Liping. Her hair was braided Tibetan style, laced with chunks of turquoise with coral, and she wore a red Chinese jacket with the sleeves torn off. They had been just torn, and the edges were frayed. She asked me if I wanted to listen. She indicated, before I speak with her, that I should listen to the children sing. This was a pre-requisite to qualify me for discussion. So I sat on the wooden studio floor beside Yang Liping. She said nothing. We listened. The children sang.

When listening to village voices, one should not sit in a chair. It is best to sit upon the floor, legs crossed, squarely and firmly in touch with the solidity beneath you. I asked Yang Liping about the philosophy of sitting cross-legged on the floor and listening to children sing.

"Regardless of philosophy or art," she explained, "this is related to the life style and environment of Yunnan, which is inseparable from nature and the very basis of life. This is not empty talk philosophy. Ethnic minorities pray to the sun. This is their philosophy. The sun is fire. They do not know about science. They just know that fire is a necessity of life. So they know that they need fire and the sun is fire. If the warmth of your personality is like fire, if your dreams are like fire, they will burn. If your love is

121

"Ethnic minorities pray to the sun...
This is their philosophy.... Dance in its essential element,
is like this ... We are not a museum."
— Yang Liping

like fire burning, you can understand the depth of this rational through the simple expression of dance."

She then pointed to the children dancing, their movement like spring flowers awakening after rain, autumn leaves blowing in cool wind. "They must retain the entire composure of their dance," she explained pointing with long thin white fingernails spreading them with her fingers like an unfolding fan. "They use their entire heart in their dance. This is not a job it is not an assignment, but an essential necessity. When they are happy, say upon getting married, they dance. When the old die and they have a funeral they dance again. When they go to the fields to plant rice seeds they sing. When they collect the harvest, they sing. Dance in its essential form is like this."

"When you were young was it your intention to become a dancer?" I asked her, pointing to the children dancing and chanting before us.

"I never went to dance school," she confided. "But in the school of life I have felt and have searched for what life is all about and come to express this. Through this there is meaning. It is not just putting music on and dancing to music. This has no meaning. I am now in the Central Ethnic Dance Troupe, my career is there. But I do not plan to stay on the stage dancing and singing. I sometimes think about my childhood, dancing alongside the river. In the village, dance is more natural. Now we must perform as a matter of work. But my composure is still that of before." She pointed to the children chanting, enveloped in village tradition. "Once you have left your roots, you have lost it. You will become light without strength, nothing behind to support you. In the end, you will not even be yourself."

"You yourself are like the children you now teach from the village. You did not study dancing but have become China's greatest modern performing dancer. You even created your own style, your own school of dance. Your Peacock Dance is famous, recognized around the world. How were you able to do this without professional training?"

"Most of mankind depends on their mouth to express feelings,

feelings toward nature, toward the things in life around them. From childhood my language was dance. If I speak my feelings toward life, you may not understand because I cannot use words to express my feelings. My most direct language is the language of motion. Some people may ask how language can become expressed in dance. I can only explain that I have found the best form of language for me."

The children continued to sing. They moved like stalks of rice in fields, being blown by a wind which finds its breath in the transition between late summer and early autumn, a time which passes by without being observed. "You must see which angle you view ethnic dance from," Yang Liping continued pointing with her long white fingernails at the girls moving in shuffles across the dance floor. "Natural environment is the basic source of life. This kind of dance which is associated with the basic elements of life is inseparable from ethnic people themselves. You must respect them and know that this is the most pure and precious of things. It is not my technique in performing the Peacock and Moon dances which has given me acclaim. It is the correct expression of those things of value to a culture. We are not a museum."

I thought about Kunming today, different from the Kunming I knew twenty years ago wandering through cobbled, tree lined streets wrapping around wood and stone shop houses of another century. Now that is gone forever. I could not find the address of Yang Liping's school because everything in this city looked the same, just blobs of cement. "But if the spirit of a culture is the basis of expression, how can expression retain in art if the culture is in danger of extinction?" I asked.

"With this kind of future we will lose this kind of natural way of living," Yang Liping sighed shaking her head. "Because now many ethnic groups do not sing, do not dance, they live in cement buildings covered with bathroom tiles, and have a modern life style. They are absorbed by many materialistic hopes. They will lose their original self. It will be gone. We must work to maintain this. But we cannot organize and force them not to lose this, because everyone will want to live a modern life. While they should protect and keep what is theirs, we cannot force them to do this. So the most rational way to do this is to quickly grasp these things which are about to be lost and find a way to keep them. In another one hundred years the villages will not exist, their people will be gone. They will be the same as ethnic Chinese. Maybe on stage or in a museum you will be able to see what they were, maybe in the end, we will only be able to save just this little."

Yang Liping explained how she had been traveling for months to the most remote villages of Yunnan Province, searching for traditional songs and dances being performed in their original state. The children she brought back to Kunming as her students were all from these villages. In fact, they were not performers at all, but village children. Their song and dance was only part of natural village life.

"They do not have any written language or technique to keep records of their dance or culture," Yang Liping explained. "How your mother teaches you is how you dance or sew. It is entirely an oral tradition. Their music has no fixed foundation. You hear them sing and it sounds so good, all four tones together in harmony. But they have no composed music, no conductor. It is not composed, but comes together as if it was. It is their own natural sound which comes together in a harmony which cannot be composed because it is their true natural expression. This is the same with their dance. Look at their clothes. It is hand sewn, with thought. There is no way to write this down and record it, because it is part of their natural life."

"Then these arts are in serious danger of being lost, and soon."

"These songs and dances are now only a few. Yunnan is not bad in that due to poor transportation, the natural life of people has been affected less than in other places. It is a border region, a mountain region. There are places where we cannot drive, so we walk. These places are better. But soon they will be gone. The government does not stop developing new roads, and it does not stop developing tourism. This creates new influences changing village life. Young men do not like wearing traditional clothes, they prefer jeans. Moreover, it requires people like me to now search and find their traditions and bring them out, to dust off what is there and make it clean again." Yang Liping pointed out that in bringing dances and songs from the villages to her dance school, she was preserving traditions intact, bringing out the best, not engaging in re-choreography. "Somebody has to do this. If there is too much dust covering the beauty of these traditions and they cannot be seen, then we have a responsibility to clean it off and make it clear. Just as if a tree is standing before you. You cannot cut it. You should only trim it so it is better looking. Take away the excessive and that tree will stand beautiful. It is also natural. It was always there. It was not cross-bred to look good."

"In a way you are rushing to preserve your own heritage," I asked. "Isn't that what this is all about?"

"In my bones I respect basic things. When you create a dance, it should naturally accord with the meaning of the dance. Internal meaning and structure of a piece of art must be in harmony with itself. There cannot be a piece of outer skin which carries a lot of unrelated things. I am strongly against this. What is modern? Tell me! It is not just wearing jeans and eating McDonalds. It is not just using an electronic music synthesizer." She pointed to village girls rehearsing on the floor before us. "You can see their dance is very modern because a modern sense of meaning is implicitly within. Look at the color of their clothing. A French fashion designer can only come this far, but cannot exceed what they have. Yes, just

125

because his color design is very modern and fashionable, you cannot dismiss what they have as ethnic and antique. The point is that their intention and ideas are modern. If so it does not matter what you are wearing. Their music is modern. The problem is can you understand it? It is not that you say you are modern or you wear something which is modern. Do you have the ability to appreciate their modernity? On stage you may be looking for modern technology and lighting effect to give color, this is only an external matter, but do they have modernity within their spirit? You cannot say they are backward. This kind of spirit we want to express and let others come to know."

"What does this spirit mean to you?"

"Healthy, composed, beautiful. This is philosophy and art which all mankind can understand. Look at the composer San Bao. His music and style is modern and beautiful. When he came to see my students perform here, he broke into tears. Why? Because he realized this was music in its original purity. He cried because upon hearing them, he discovered the beauty of music, how it moves others. Dance was originally a total expression, not a fulfillment of duty. He has seen too many performances which were for the sake of completing an assignment, seen too many performances for money, for a purpose. But this moved him because it was purely for spirit, expression of inner self."

"Yes, San Bao said, if I come to Yunnan in Search of Shangri-la, I must first search out you!"

"From childhood my grandmother taught me — of course she did not use the term Shangri-la — as our ethnic group uses the term Mo Li Ye Na. Later, after I grew up, I understood. In fact the idea is the same. It is a question of differences in language. Westerners call it Shangri-la. Chinese call it a 'Peach Garden beyond the realm'. At Lijiang's Jade Dragon Snow Mountain they talk about a 'third world', Shangri-la. Many young boys and girls are not afraid to die. They actually believe in dying, because it is natural phenomena. After love, the couples will climb the Jade Dragon Snow Mountain and jump off to their death, because they are going into the third realm of Jade Dragon, to Shangri-la. When they go to the third realm of Shangri-la they believe that this

126

realm is the best, so they are not afraid to die. After death they will go to an even better place. They are romantic. They are not like Chinese who feel that after death you become dust and it is sad. They are not like this. They believe that after a person dies, they will go to the third realm. It is very romantic. It is not that they are not afraid, they are idealistic. Just like Tibetans turning a prayer wheel. After death they will return and it will be better. This hope allows them to go through the realities of this world with happiness. Look at the Tibetans. So what if life is somewhat bitter? Because the environment they live in is harsh, the air thin, no oxygen, freezing cold, it is a difficult place to live. So you must have hope, your own hope, like Shangri-la. If your hope is built on this, you will not be afraid of death. They are not afraid of the bitterness in their life. The future will be better. They live in a dreamlike world, not a clear precise world like yours. You want to find out precisely what and where Shangri-la is, to define it and tell others. But they are in a dream and for them this dream is Shangri-la."

"You are also a Bai ethnic minority, from Dali, right?" I asked. "Some say Dali is Shangri-la. Others say Lijiang or Zhongdian. Regardless, is Shangri-la here in Yunnan? What do you really think?"

"Our Bai ethnic minority believe in every person's soul, so there is a culture of wizardry, communicating with the dead, with the soul. They know there is lots of empty space for communication, only in the spirit, in the ideal. Why are Yunnan people so gentle? You must ask yourself this question. Because our environment is so nice, clear water, green mountains, great natural outdoors, so their life style is very happy. They can sing, dance and culture is rich. They won't get angry and frustrated. On the mountains you will often see a woman carrying huge bundles of scrap wood, bigger than the woman herself, climbing the mountain trail, twisting threads for spindling busily being sewn in her hands as she walks, with the naturalness with which we might drive and use the mobile telephone. She accepts this and does not have any anger toward this life. She thinks that since I have such a life, I must give birth, have many children and let life multiply. It is a very natural attitude toward life."

"Then you follow a philosophy of a natural attitude toward life,

127

both in your life and dance. Is that right? The naturalness of your dance is an expression of your philosophy toward life?"

"One must first 'sense' and then 'realize'. Many people have sense but no realization. For instance, in dance, you can say you studied a lot, you watched a lot, you feel that dance is good, but when you try yourself, you cannot express yourself. In such a case there is sensation but no realization. Your body cannot realize expression. You can only feel good but not express it. Many people have gone to many universities and have lots knowledge and experience, but they cannot write a good novel. Many students have studied lots of dance, but cannot dance well. To realize or awaken is realization, to have vision to see and then to do. It is not that you can only see but not do. This effects dance, fashion, even film. Does that camera focus capture that particular meaning intended? This is important. Can it completely express it? Ask yourself! Dance is like that. This is something which cannot be taught. It can only be within your own self. If you practice without desire or feeling, then it is useless. If you have desire and feeling, and you have realization, then you can achieve it."

Feeling, comprehension, realization, I wondered to myself? "Maybe then the search for Shangri-la is not about a place, but about feeling and comprehension?" I was more confused than enlightened.

"If your intention is to find Shangri-la but your way is all messed up, if you hurt or kill people on the way, then how can you find Shangri-la? From your heart there is no Shangri-la but only from your mouth you say you are looking for it, you want to find a happy life, but you do not create that happy life, don't you realize that a happy life must be created. There are two directions. One is realism, while another is your spirit and attitude. If you think I must definitely find a spiritual Shangri-la and make a very ideal atmosphere, the result being what you do is all messed up, then that spirit is false. You do not have any belief, so you do not know what Shangri-la is all about. You talk about living happy days, but you don't go out and create a happy life, then you will not be happy. This is the difference between realism and spirit. If you want to fix Shangri-la at any particular place, then you will lose the meaning of Shangri-la, because Shangri-la is without place. You cannot use

128

one place or one product to represent Shangri-la. Therefore, Shangri-la cannot be said to be in Zhongdian, it cannot be fixed in Lijiang, because Lijiang is quite beautiful and people say that this could possibly be the place of Shangri-la, that book's author was searching for a lost Shangri-la. No place can represent Shangri-la. Only spirit can. Lijiang and Zhongdian are Shangri-la. Are they the most beautiful places? They are only places where the natural environment has been protected quite well, so you might think that they are Shangri-la."

"So you are saying neither Lijiang nor Zhongdian is Shangri-la?" I asked quite taken back by her words.

"To really find a place, this is meaningless," she warned, raising one thin white fingernail, unfolding the other delicate fingers, spreading her hand like a white fan. "We can only search for it. We can seek it in what is beautiful. Already from perspective of spirit, we have found it. In Yunnan there are many places where you can feel Shangri-la and have this feeling. But to say you can completely find it is impossible. The Peach Garden of Chinese legend does not exist. The movement of dance can achieve a beautiful appearance from dance moves. Because of the effect dance has, you can be affected. Music and clothing might be beautiful. If beautiful then this is Shangri-la. There are writers who have come back and said there is no Shangri-la, as it has been destroyed. So they can only go and look further."

So I went to look further. I would follow her directions to see for myself, traveling to Lijiang, then to Zhongdian, the two counties claiming to be Shangri-la. When I left Yang Liping's studio, I could hear lingering voices of village children. They were still singing. As I traveled to Lijiang, to Zhongdian, hitchhiking along network of roads which wound past villages, through valleys and up into mountains, I could still hear their echo clinging to my memory, haunting internal recesses of meditation upon smooth lake waters waiting to be touched. The purity of village children chanting had been captured for a moment and held in Yang Liping's vision, a call from wilderness, the crying of a purple moon in rain. I was reminded to stop for a moment before sacred snow capped mountains, wait, listening for snow to melt.

# Rock Concert in Rain

I arrived at Jade Dragon Snow Mountain Music Festival. When the rock concert had begun, it was already dark. There was no snow, only rain. I could not listen to snow melt because the music was too loud. The music was being drowned in rain. It rained throughout the concert, but this did not prevent a huge crowd from climbing to the mountain's foot already 3 000 meters above sea level, listening to music. The rain created a special effect forcing stage lights to split into smithereens of fractured kaleidoscope light against puncturing rain drops which left performers and audience soaked. I wandered through the crowd, through music, through rain. As kids and police danced the effect was surreal explaining why so many had come out for the concert, despite so much rain.

In the morning, it was sunny, fresh, feeling clarity after rain. I called Kaiser Kuo, one of the first and maybe last of China's hard core rock stars. Founder of legendary rock band Tang Dynasty, he was now heading another band named after another dynasty, Spring and Autumn. We met in the old city of Lijiang for coffee. We met by a river. The river ran past cafes giving the place an air of Venice. The coffee was dark Yunnan. It had that pungent oily smell of Yunnan hillside slopes cut by hands of ethnic tribes wearing clothes passed from grandmother, to mother, to daughter, and the smell of rain. I stared into the cup of coffee looking for Shangri-la. I guess I was not looking hard enough. So I asked Kaiser where I should look next.

"How did your concert go last night?" I asked him.

"Extremely well, except for the rain. We were nearly rained out. The whole carpet on the stage was soggy, felt like electricity currents were running on me the entire time. It was like having a leaking battery tied to you. But the crowd was really enthusiastic. We were sort of the only band left with long hair. Even though Spring and Autumn is a new group, we still carry the fame of my old band Tang Dynasty."

"Many are calling this music festival the Woodstock of China, is it?"

"I do not think it is going to be the seminal defining event in the musical life of a whole generation. But it is a start. People flew in from all over China. There was a huge group from Kunming and Sichuan as well. Sure the Beijing rock crowd was also here. There are only a few towns in China which have become centers for rock music. One of these cities is Kunming. Another is Chengdu. People fall in love with these towns. There is something really great and cool. Beijing of course has always been China's main center for Rock and Roll. In fact, the entire idea for this music festival was started by Cui Jian, a great start," Kaiser thought for a moment while staring into his coffee cup. "Unfortunately, the big attraction, the snow mountain, could not be seen because of the rain."

"Why is China's music scene drawn to Lijiang to hold a Woodstock style festival? Will Lijiang become the next rock and roll town in China?" I asked. "Is there some kind of search for inspiration in Shangri-la taking place now among China's art circles?"

"Frankly, I am not sure the Lijiang musical festival itself is the manifestation of this tendency, and I don't think Lijiang is going to become a center of rock. Like the other things in China, the Shangri-la idea has great attraction for the west, which is the whole thing behind this New Age Music, there is a sort of mystic Orientalism giving rise to white Buddhism — American Buddhists and European Buddhists. This is something which has had roots way back before Hilton's Shangri-la or Lost Horizon. The Rosicrucians for example was one of the European mystical sects fascinated with Tibet. They sought this mystical land, believing that Christ was re-incarnated or re-born there. After this Christian infection of Tibet, I am not sure what it is, a lot of westerners,

are crazy for anything about the Himalayas, they really take in this hocus pocus stuff, the jewelry, the chanting music, the Thankas."

"Is this just an optical illusion of Christianity? Maybe the ideas behind Christ's teachings originally came from Buddha and Christianity just recycled re-incarnation as a concept?"

"I am really not going that far. I am not a scholar of religious history, so I do not really know the direction of transmission. In fact, you see a lot of images in Buddhism, like Guan Yin or Bodhisattvas which look very much like Virgin Mary or saints for example. I do not know what is the direction of transmission, whether it is just illusion between Christianity I can not see. I see in the west a lot of people who for good sound science reasons reject western traditions, but lose all sense of that when approaching eastern philosophy. They suddenly embrace anything that comes from the misty east. That is what is sad to me. It is sort of cheap thing I think in some ways."

"In a way we now have the emergence of 'Shangri-la chic', right?"

"Now in China you see figures emerging like 'Dadawa' whose real name is Zhu Zheqin, an ethnic Han musician, who has really created something which is right out from the Yunnan - Tibet plateau. You can see young Chinese are now wearing batik clothes, silver jewelry, listening to new age music. The sad irony is that much of the value in this culture is coming to China via the west. It is a type of fashion. It was not long ago that you would never see Chinese people wearing a high mandarin collar, Chinese buttons, lime green, the Shanghai look, until it became popular in the west. What was suddenly running down the catwalk in Milan, Paris, and Tokyo, suddenly came back in China and in force, an ironic boomerang effect. Likewise, a town like Lijiang suddenly becomes popular again. I hate to use the term again, but it is almost Orientalism being re-imported with eastern people re-embracing their supposed heritage because it became popular in the west for some reason. A lot of reasons for what you see happening lies in this."

I stared into my coffee cup thinking about what Kaiser was saying. For a moment I stopped looking for Shangri-la in the coffee cup,

133

and instead asked Kaiser, "Westerners are trying to find Shangri-la through Buddhism, music, or dress, or fashion. But doesn't the search for Shangri-la go deeper than that?" Coffee yet to be drunk was getting cold in the crisp morning air.

"I am not sure," Kaiser thought for a moment, now staring into his coffee cup. "There are many people familiar with Shangri-la in the west, even if they have only heard of a utopian place where people do not age. Yes, there are many people who come here searching for Shangri-la. But in reality, the westerners and visitors who come here are not really searching for Shangri-la. They are searching for beautiful scenery, ethnic minorities with beautiful costumes, and the gorgeous architecture. The town is absolutely beautiful in spite of what has happened in the past few years with tourists overcrowding the place, becoming like Venice where the river canals are lined with parallel souvenir shops. But the real irony is that most people who come here are still big groups of tourists following some guy holding a yellow flag. They are not going to see the charming little villages. They are going to stay in those white bathroom tile and blue glass hotels. They need infrastructure. They need to sing Karaoke. Sure for experimental experience you can go and have a Tibet barley mash with Yak meat if you want. But there is always pizza around. Look, in Dali there is a whole street called 'Foreigners' Street'. It happens everywhere in this region that opens to tourism."

"It is extremely ironic that three counties have been in dispute over which will use the name 'Shangri-la'. There are also three provinces which all want to be known as Shangri-la at the same time," I had already traveled from Tibet, through Qinghai and now was in Yunnan's Lijiang. Soon I would go to Zhongdian. I was basically making the rounds of all places competing for the title of the "real" Shangri-la. "It's all driven by the material objective of tourist dollars, not any spiritual objective of what Shangri-la is supposed to be."

"Can you have what they call in World Bank lexicon 'sustainable development' and at the same time keep the culture?"

"Yes, on one hand things have changed here dramatically within just a few years. All these quaint little guest houses now have

ADSL internet access and the cafes are knocking out banana pancakes and apple pie to back-packers. On the other hand, this is livelihood for the people living here, so there is nothing wrong with Shangri-la business.

I would do the same thing if I were they. The reality for them is that Shangri-la is something which draws western tourism. To them it does not have anything to do with their culture."

"Aside from the tourists and back-packers, let's look at the music concert. What are the artists trying to seek by coming here?"

"The artists are trying to seek audiences. They are obviously interested in this field. If you walk inside through any mid-sized American town you will see the new age shops with crystal from Atlantis, tarot cards, and all that stuff. It personally makes me want to vomit. I've seen this before. One of my friends in Beijing, who runs a nice little bar next to Hou Hai always plays a New Age Music CD. One day I took a look at the CD cover and it had a little sticker on it saying 'Wood Protector Mirror', with a little Ba Gua eight-gram cheesy oriental mirror attached in the middle of it. This is all cheesy Chinese. The names of the songs were like Mountain, Cloud, and River. I looked at it and the guy got some Tibetan Buddhist symbol on the cover. Then I noticed his actual name is something like Hydrick Vongroomon, some German guy. He is trying to make something out of this new age chic. It makes me sick."

"Why does it make you sick?"

"Clearly it is just an attempt to milk this new age trend for whatever it is worth, to grab middle aged people who are looking for some meaning in life. Yes it's an illusion. Maybe it's not even that. It's a kind of vulnerability which has made them accept without a real reflection mystic east philosophy while rejecting the religious traditions handed on to them by their parents."

"So in a way westerners are turning away from western values, turning to eastern values and looking for the instant noodle, Shangri-la in a package, made easy. This in turn calls for the commercializing of Shangri-la in a way which in the end may make Shangri-la not so Shangri-la. Is that what's happening?" I thought

135

for a moment about what I had just said, staring into a now almost empty cup of bitter Yunnan coffee. "If so, then what is Shangri-la?"

"It's a fictional notion drummed up by a guy named James Hilton from a book he was writing. It might or might not be predicated on a real physical location, possibly near Zhongdian, Lijiang or near Dali."

"So it's not an overall concept of Qinghai-Tibetan plateau culture?"

"Yes I think it's an amalgamation of the very features of that, or a westerner's imagination of what those features should be. Yes, sure, it also includes a repackaging of utopian ideas which have always been around. The Chinese have the idea of an eternal peach garden, or Penglai island. Qingshihuang, the founding emperor of China sent a mission abroad with 500 young virgin boys and 500 young virgin girls looking for this island. They found Japan instead, and stayed there."

"When did Hilton write his book 'Lost Horizon' introducing the Shangri-la idea?"

"In the 1930s, almost 70 years ago, and suddenly there is a new resurgence of interest in finding Shangri-la or coming to this region. This is due to a convergence of two things, which ironically are in conflict. China is opening up, wanting tourists' dollars and western materialism. The new age phenomena in the west, seeks to achieve a higher plane of human consciousness in finding and practicing a set of non-materialist Asian values now rejected in Asia, being replaced by western materialism."

"Then is Shangri-la just an illusion, as soon as you go and seek it, it disappears?" At this point I was beginning to become disillusioned.

"Sure. It never existed in the first place. There isn't a real place. There may be some real article talking about it but it's a meaningless idea. There are many other places like Kunlun Mountain or Penglai Mountain. Every culture has their own secret places where people never age, everyone is peaceful and happy. Native Americans had a lot of ideas like this. Indian culture has things like this in South Asia. In European civilization too we have Thomas Moore, we have Plato's Republic. These are not real places. They are only in your mind. But it never hurts to keep looking."

I had to keep looking. The snows were melting in rain. They were rushing down a creek in Lijiang, beneath delicate stone bridges, past banana pancake cafes lining old canals twisting along narrow alleyways. A long line of Taiwan tourists were walking on ancient stones searching in an orderly manner, behind the shadow of a young Beijing girl in a yellow baseball cap, carrying a yellow flag. She was leading the tourists to Shangri-la.

Shangri-La in a Cup of Tea

I followed the river, crossed a bridge and lost the yellow flag disappearing around a corner of an old stone wall which looked as if it would collapse but would not because it had not over at least five centuries. Stepping up from the street I walked through the door of a quaint little café filled with Tibetan antiques tucked into the wall of a side street by a river running through Lijiang. "So is this your cafe?" I asked.

"Yes, it is called Dadawa Cafe," replied Zhu Zheqin, pop star known as "Dadawa" to the world. "But Dadawa Cafe belongs to everybody as well." She explained. I was offered a cup of tea.

"So, you mean it is for everyone?" I stared into the empty blue cracked ceramic tea cup on the table between us. Someone had gone to get hot water.

"Yeah," she replied. "When you look for Dadawa Cafe, you think you are looking for me, but it belongs to, you know, whoever is looking." Tea was poured.

"Dadawa," I asked. "Tell me, where exactly is Shangri-la?" I held the tea cup. It was now warm.

"When I first came here, I think it was in early 1995, and people who worked with me were all talking about Tibet, talking about some kind of ideal place. We kept walking, and we kept traveling, wanting to find something else."

"How did the journey begin?"

"Because I was born in Guangzhou, a really noisy city in south China, for me everything there seemed limited. When I grew up, as a university student, I just felt things were boring. Because everyday you have one routine, going to work, studying, talking with people, having a drink with friends in a bar, no more. We listen to some music and we read some books, but this is all life offered me, and then my heart began to fly, because when I was a kid, I had something in my mind, just growing, growing within me. So after graduating from the university, I started to travel. First, of course, I traveled around Guangdong. My family gave me great support, because they knew I had my own world that they could see. When I was a kid, they give me more freedom. I started to travel around Guangdong and Shandong more far away, farther away. In 1992, I had a chance to work in a TV festival, in Sichuan. I met a composer who had been in Sichuan for many years composing music, and he was greatly interested in Tibetan music and culture. He helped me collect some Tibetan folk songs over many years. After, we finished a song called Yellow Children. It was from that point we started our journey to Tibet."

"What were you searching for on that journey?"

"We felt kind of lost. We did not know the things before early times, for instance where we came from? That is the common question for everyone when we grow up. We just wanted to know where we came from. All things in the world will become just like that in the end so we just wanted to find it out. I had a heavy feeling for some time when I lived in the city. We stopped believing anymore. I thought everything is not true. This feeling followed me for many years. I just got confused, just the faces, the lives around me in a city. I always got confused and I did not know why? So in my heart I just felt so lost, I wanted to build my own world. First I started music, and art. Then I started my journey as soon as I grew up and I kept looking, and found a totally different experience when in southwestern China, because of the culture, the atmosphere, the way people live. It is all new for me. It really

touched my heart."

"Then you really weren't searching for something," I queried. My tea cup was half empty. "Rather you were being called. Is that right?"

"Yes, I do believe my heart, my strong sense of feeling, keeps calling me, calling me, calling me. And then I travel, on the way to everywhere, I received a simple kind of peace from my heart. And started to have conversations with mountains, we can talk. That is not real for most people. They will call this a laughable experience. But for me it is really true."

"When you talk with a mountain what happens, what do you say, what does the mountain say?" I stared into the tea cup, this time carefully.

"I am just moved, deeply moved, and then they can tell me lots of real knowledge of the world of our coming, and relationships between people, and nature and the world, and life style. Great, suddenly I find a new world. And now if you want me to tell you what Shangri-la is, I have the confidence to tell you, I know this."

"What is it?" I asked leaning over listening intently. A thin flame from a candle melting slowly on the table in front of Dadawa lit her face, reflecting gently in her eyes. "Tell me what is Shangri-la?" A drop of wax dripped downward, settling upon the Tibetan brass candlestick below. I had a sense of the deliberate looking into flame melting candlestick.

"Shangri-la is in people, the ideal world of our mind," Dadawa explained exuding with confidence of someone who has found what he was searching for, but was continuing to search for what was already found, that sense of knowing what you are looking for, taking it away once it is found, and then looking for it again. "But it seems that it is not a real world. But if you keep going in that way to find the way in your mind, you will make things come true. It is something you think you realize. It is untrue, but if you keep going

141

that is the true way to go regardless of distance. The real Shangri-la is in you, yourself. That is why I am living in this world."

"So how can one find it?"

She blinked as she looked into the flame. "First step, you must have an ideal world in your mind. That is really important for people. But the ideal world for each person is different. You have your own mind, your idea, your country. For everyone this is different. Refuse to make all things just like one thing. This is the difference. Everybody can have their own world in their own mind. But this is only the first step, right? Remember, you have to keep going."

"So you kept going, right? Did you find your Shangri-la?"

"Of course," the small café echoed with her enthusiasm. A young Naxi boy came over and poured more tea into the half empty cup. The cup overflowed, dripping tea on the old wooden table between us. It seeped into cracks which had emerged when releasing moisture some time ago, when nobody could remember, maybe before the wood had become a table. "We are living a true world, but it is not our ideal world," she went on. "Everyday, every moment there are lots of things which make you sometimes feel upset. Sometimes feel really difficult. You then have to choose, to keep going, but sometimes you will find a little shining light, like this candle, just a little shining flame, and then you just keep going. I think there is nothing which can not come true. If you have confidence, if you have a pure heart, everything can come true. I believe that."

"What about the Jade Dragon Snow Mountain Music Festival which you sang at yesterday. Many young people came here from all over China. Did they come to the Jade Dragon Snow Mountain for a music festival, or do you think they are searching for something else?"

"I think the reason they come here is to communicate. Because in China this is the first time we have had a really big event in the

Jade Dragon Snow Mountain. Young kids always want to find somewhere to express their feelings, so there is something about a music festival which seems similar everywhere, but I think there is still something different here."

"The search for Shangri-la seems to be an international trend. Some call it 'new age fusion' life style, others a re-action to globalization, maybe anti-globalization values." I drank some tea from the overfull cup. "What do you think?"

"I think the problem is not globalization, the problem is we have limited knowledge of how humanity should develop. So I just say everybody can have their own world. I feel my music and my life style is mine. I think everybody knows I am a Chinese, I am a singer. But my life is not so similar with the other fashionable artists. Because I have my value of life, I do not think I have to follow the fashionable rules. So I have my own world, and I think as I keep going the whole world belongs to me. Sometimes I open it to anyone who wants to listen and through my music can communicate love, beliefs, and my whole world. Everybody should have their own world. That is really important. That is why you come here, to the earth. You are just a guest here, to find the real meaning of life."

I took a sip of tea and watched the leaves unfolding in heat reflected against blue ceramic, and thought about what Dadawa had just said. I was still looking for answers. "What about so-called New Age Music, does this capture the essence of a new fusion life style, or this new craving trend, call it what you want, to search for Shangri-la?"

"I think the problem is here, that is why my music is greatly influenced from traditional, oriental music, religion, and culture together. But we use new technology to synthesize it. You still must express yourself. Likewise, I do not care whether people try to label my music saying I belong to this type or that type. At first I think my music is myself, and something in my heart. I think my music just express something, because my music moves

143

freely. We do not have the burden of what kind of music we have to follow. I would like to call my music 'Dadawa' music. Because I am not new age, new age is a kind of background music."

"Some people say that your music speaks out for the environment, for culture, for preservation of the Qinghai-Tibetan plateau. At the same time environment and ethnic life styles are in danger of being bulldozed by development. Can we talk about your music in the context of 'sustainable development'?" I took another sip. A single tea leaf spun in concentric circles. I watched the leaf and listened to Dadawa.

"We come from China," she explained. "We express our feeling to all of world including our people. In our culture, we have had really elegant periods in history, and very harsh and painful periods as well. Just like someone's scar. You always show it again, show it again. I am a new generation, each time it really deeply hurts me. It makes me really sad. I want to see hope. But it is not our aim. That is what I want to do. I met lots of people in Yunnan, in Tibet. They can keep their culture, and they also have a good life. I love them. I think it is kind of selfish if you want someone just remain poor, with no medicine. I am a modern person. I do not want all people to go back 300 years ago. It is impossible. But we are living here. We have to build our own world. We still have a way to go. We do not have one way. Computer is one way but it is just a tool. Because I have traveled a lot here, I love the children and people here. I want them to have a good life. But also at the same time, they can keep their culture and traditions. I think it is difficult. They are trying to do that. But it is difficult, because you have to have some kind of knowledge and technology all the way to help this happen."

"What has given you inspiration in your search for Shangri-la?"

"Because I am a human being, I am living here, living in the world, I love the earth. It is the true experience. I came here, it is the only way. For everybody Shangri-la is different. For me in my heart, I have my own Shangri-la. I think it is different."

144

"What is it for you?"

"It is just an ideal world, but in this ideal world, where everything is real, just like my life style. I like music, travel, reading, just enjoying, sometimes just keeping silent. I believe life is just like floating water. It will keep going. Shangri-la in my life is a pure heart, when you love people, communicate with people. When you feel sad, when you feel happy, it is just pure. You have no conditions. For me Shangri-la is the real world. Remember the Buddhist saying, 'share with others'."

I left Dadawa Café where I had been searching for Shangri-la in a cup of tea which somebody poured but forgot to take notice of. If anyone realized that Shangri-la was somewhere in that cup of tea, that is if they had the slightest idea that a round blue cracked piece of ceramic tea cup possessed such a powerful uniting force among people as a vision of Shangri-la, would they rush back after pouring tea, empty the tea in a river outside Dadawa Café, and look for Shangri-la inside the tea cup?

I think most people would not take the time to actually pay attention to the depth or width or precise measurement of tea arising from a tea cup after tea is poured. They would dismiss such observation as merely vapor. Moreover, they would not bother to throw tea in a river and then look for Shangri-la in the tea cup, or river. As Dadawa said, "life is just like floating water. It will keep going."

So I left Dadawa after drinking the cup of tea and walked down ancient cobbled streets of Lijiang which wound along the river where tea should have been dumped and dispersed. It was in this process of walking through the narrow winding stone slab streets of Lijiang that I became aware of the enormous dispersion which can be emitted through this very simple act of throwing out a cup of tea. I began to wander back to Dadawa Café to look for the cup without the tea which had been dispersed. Dadawa had already left. The cup was being washed. I realized that when searching for Shangri-la in a cup of tea, one must look carefully.

Half Full
HALF EMPTY
ZEN tea cup

145

# Misty Valleys

I left Lijiang in the afternoon. The sun was setting and the shape of shadows fit in between slabs of stone. They became thin black lines which cut deeply between rocks like black rivers cutting canyons through eons of time, until one becomes clear that they are only walking across stone slabs laid cross-wise like a checkerboard in a street by a Naxi stone cutter who laid them two hundred years ago and went in the other direction but was not lost because he had laid the streets and tiny stone bridges which he would walk upon, and cross, when he left.

I left the old city of Lijiang, and walked. I crossed a valley and climbed a hill. Upon reaching the top I looked back down on the valley. It rested along a river which split in several places forming creeks like the branch of a tree which has smaller branches each of which has leaves. And when leaves fall off they swirl in the wind in concentric circles until they come to the valley. Sometimes they rest upon the water and flow down a river which split in several places forming creeks like the branch of a tree which has smaller branches each of which has leaves. This is the way the valley can be understood, rich with green in many cooling shades, water which flows nourishing the green. It is important to understand a valley before you have completely passed through.

In the valley there was a village. The village houses were quiet in late afternoon. The Naxi people of the village had come back to their houses. Their animals were tucked into corals for the evening. The valley with quiet houses gave a sense of collective cohesion, not disbursement. The people who live in the valley were content. They did not realize that I was sitting on a hill looking at their

146

147

valley, or moments before I had passed through. From this perspective one can feel the contentment of valley living oozing upward through various shades of late afternoon green waiting to be forgotten by an orange setting sun.

I was tired and climbed further to a crest of road which wound past the valley. Now it would be late and the road to Zhongdian long. So I hitchhiked until a jeep stopped. It was driven by a Tibetan who spoke good Chinese. He had long hair like a Navaho Indian and wore turquoise around his neck, tucked under an old sweater. He suggested I wear a sweater as the night ahead would become cool when the orange green became blue.

I hopped into the back of his jeep and we climbed into blue which became darkness. On the side of the mountain road I could not hear anything except the rush of a great river, the torrent of force pouring from mountain snows below a winding road into valleys of green. I could not see the river but only hear the power of water pouring from snow capped ridges across round obtuse stones. I kept hearing the sound of water rushing through recesses of my memory and forgot that I had slept across a sequence of hours when the Tibetan woke me pointing to a large Tibetan house tucked in a valley which breathed dark purple in the early morning hours. This is where I would stay, as the journey was completed.

Journey completed? This did not make sense for some reason. I checked into a two story Tibetan house which had been converted into a guest house and stood on the wooden balcony looking out across a valley of purple moonlight. Cold evaporated against the release of heat from a cup of yak butter tea and I clasped the cup close to my chest to feel the warmth observing what appeared to be a white pagoda rising from the crest of a nearby hillside. I was now in Zhongdian County, otherwise known by the name "Shangri-la". But had I really found "Shangri-la"? In the morning as the sun rose, I drank more yak butter tea and climbed the white pagoda.

In James Hilton's book "Lost Horizon" he describes Shangri-la as a valley surrounded by snow capped mountains on all sides, grasslands with yak and sheep, all kinds of ethnic groups with different religious beliefs living in harmony, and golden temple

pavilions touching the sky. I looked out over the green valley, leaning against the white pagoda. There were other pagodas in the distance, and the temple roofs behind me touched the sky. Ultimately the search for Shangri-la had brought me here to Zhongdian County, now officially known as Shangri-la County after a long hard dispute with other counties in the Qinghai-Tibetan plateau region which all claimed to be Shangri-la in anticipation of the tourist spending which would pour in on top of the name, branding. But here I was in Shangri-la and I thought for a moment that maybe I had escaped this wild addiction to dollars through my own search for Shangri-la.

I sat at the pagoda and looked out over the valley. Children came to turn prayer wheels. They wore different kinds of Tibetan clothes. In their simplicity, they were a pageant of color. Turning the wheels for them was not a religious experience. It was a game. The wheels turned. The children laughed. They surrounded me as I sat there writing. I asked them if this was Shangri-la. They just laughed. I kept writing. Then when their laughter turned to mountain mist, I looked up. They had already run away.

There are valleys hidden in the mist. You cannot find the valleys because of mist. But you must assure yourself that they are present, waiting to be found. This requires your mind to be centered in situations of dispersion. Some call it belief. Others call it certainty. When the sun rises the mist departs. The valleys become apparent, real. You may enter the valleys and look for remaining mist. It will have already scattered.

Follow the tiny creek which follows contours of the land, of small rocks which have been carried by the creek and left there when its waters continued down the slope. This slope is the home of wood cutters. They are simple mountain folk who live off the slope. They cut wood. They have no other trade or source of income. They live in tiny log cabins made of wood they have already cut. They weave their own clothes, have few possessions, and ask for nothing from anybody. When I came to the woodcutters' home, he offered me fresh warm milk. It was not pasteurized and pure. It did not come from a carton, cellophane box, or prepared formula. It was very fresh and warm. He was fifty five years old but looked

149

more like thirty. Strapped on his back was a grandson. Two grand daughters played on the floor. I sat in his log cabin by a red fire and drank the milk which had been boiled in a thin aluminum pot over the fire. The two girls sat beside me with curious eyes. They watched me drink warm milk. I asked the wood cutter if he had ever heard of Shangri-la. To my surprise, he said "yes".

Of course, he explained, "Shangri-la is here."

"Here?"

"Yes, here."

I looked at the log cabin around me. I could see outside through the cracks and knew that this would be a cold place to live in the winter, even fall or spring. The floor was dirt. There were hardly any possessions. A Tibetan dog barked furiously outside, irritated by my presence. The grandchildren stared at me drinking milk. And I realized that in the poverty which this wood cutter found in his surroundings, he was in Shangri-la.

"Don't you want to live in the city?" I asked the wood cutter.

"Why live in the city? The conditions are not sufficient. Here is mountain. I have the mountain. The mountain is mine to live on. I have little in possessions, but a lot here is mine. See the mountain. It has snow in winter, colors in fall, flowers in spring, and in summer I can cut wood. If I want change, I will move to another mountain. What does the city have to offer? Shangri-la is here. This spot is Shangri-la."

Niyma Tsering's words came back to me like a gunshot from the rooftop of Johkang Temple in Lhasa ringing across the mountains, deserts and plains I had crossed over the weeks behind me, ringing like a proverbial echo through misty valleys of Yunnan, into the recesses of my mind as I sat before this simple wood cutter. "I have money, I have factory, but I am not happy, even beggars are more relaxed than me," Niyma Tsering had said. I could see his saffron robed shadow in a blazing Tibetan sun, pointing his finger upwards to heaven, then downwards to earth as he said. "This is the search for Shangri-la."

# Saving Shangri-la

I found Uttara Sarkar Crees of Gyalthang Dzong eco-tourism hotel tucked in a valley surrounded by mountains, which generated energy of a kind that can only be found in a quiet valley where intrusion is minimal, an occasional Tibetan, tying a jinfan prayer flag to a stone on a mountain. It was this sense of oneness with her environment which Uttara projected in her speech and movement. She was now dedicating her entire existence to developing eco-tourism in the Qinghai-Tibetan plateau area, sharing her decades of experience with local government officials there, in an attempt to change people's thinking. It was her goal to create awareness for what they had, and should keep.

"I am from India. I grew up in Africa and lived in Africa and India," she explained pouring a cup of ginger Indian tea. "Then I was living in Nepal, operating an eco-tourism consultancy. I traveled all around the Himalayas right from Karachi to western Tibet. I never stopped for a rest. In 1987 I was invited by a Tibetan friends' family to Shangri-la and at that time I lived for two months and just loved it. After 1987 I wanted to come back here because it was just so wonderful. As I was saying I had seen the entire Himalayas all over but I had not seen such beauty as I found here. It fascinated me and I wanted to come back and explore more. Eventually in the early 1990s my husband and I came back and received a wonderful welcome from the government here. Anything we wanted to do was fine. And of course my interest was eco-tourism, so we decided to come and set-up a traditional hotel that would offer Tibetan hospitality and start an eco-tourism operation."

"Eco-tourism?" I had heard this term many times. Clearly it was in vogue. "Can you tell me what that really means?" I began looking into the cup of ginger tea convinced this time that Shangri-la must be somewhere inside.

"It is culturally and environmentally sensitive tourism. And tourism that can establish certain management standards in relation with places in order to protect the culture and environmental aspects of that area. It also must be sustainable. So these are basically the general principles that we follow in developing eco-tourism."

The principles were simple, but clear. In fact eco-tourism does not involve all of the complicated management models of the tourist industry which you need to go to tourism management school to learn and require years in the hotel industry to acquire such skills of management. Rather eco-tourism as a concept, required a sense of common sense, something most people lose when they go to management school. It also required establishing a philosophical platform for one's life style, and then living it. "How is the eco-tourism concept going down in China? Is it received well here in Yunnan?"

"I think it took time but they are now very receptive. In China, vast numbers of people travel. They travel together in very big groups. That is what they think is good tourism. But it will take time to slowly understand the fact that tourism creates impact. It brings bad things as well as good things. If a management is put into a place for the purpose of meeting the impact then we are on our way to developing good tourism, quality tourism."

"But by encouraging tourism into an area like Shangri-la, won't it in the end endanger what we have. Maybe those searching for Shangri-la will come here and find the opposite of what they were looking for, because so many came before."

"Absolutely, there is very real danger of that. I mean you see here in this grassland right in front of the hotel, we have at least 60 different varieties of wild flowers. If you were here in May, at

152

the end of May, through the middle of June to the third week of June, you would not believe how many wild flowers there are here. We bring many botanic groups and they spend days just here, all impressed with the numbers of flowers. We have also very rare flowers too. Just imagine in a place like Bika Lake and Shudo Lake where hundreds of people are beginning to visit. If they trip all over each year, flowers will be less and less. This is the point of eco-tourism as a concept. You have guidelines in place. So the flowers and trees remain protected. There is no damage to the environment, or at least minimum damage that can be reversed. Otherwise the very thing that guests come to see will be gone in five to ten years. And garbage, the big problem with huge tourism is garbage. People throw their cola bottles out of bus windows, instant noodle packages are thrown out wherever they go. So there have to be guidelines and education in place to keep Shangri-la."

"But the local government is opening this region up to tourism," I said feeling warmth of ginger tea emanating across a field of wild flowers, we were sitting in. "They are quite excited about the prospects, more flights and all that."

"So far we only have very few direct flights. There are two flights out of Kunming, one flight a week out of Chengdu and one flight a week out of Lhasa, so there is not the huge numbers of tourists you see at other sites in China that are very popular. But the point is ten people who are educated or who are sensitive will create less impact than one who is not. There are people who throw trash every place they go, they will take their picnic lunch and leave everything behind, plastic will fly everywhere. That will infect the environment."

"How," I asked, "do you disinfect the increasing effect of more tourism?"

"There are tourists who will barge into local homes and not be respectful, or will buy everything they see. So education for visitors is very important. Here we have guidelines for each visitor which we ask them to follow. And we teach our guides to ensure that these guidelines are followed. Hopefully next step will be to educate the drivers who are often with guests without guides, to say please don't throw things outside, leave them in the car. I will dispose of them properly. Very simple management is needed, but there must be wide education across the tourism industry."

"What is it that has kept you here in Shangri-la? You have lived in so many beautiful parts of the Himalayas, but in the end came here to stay. Why?"

"To be completely truthful, I used to suffer from asthma a lot. But since I have come here I am very healthy. I don't take any medicine. I am both mentally and physically healthy here. People are just wonderful here, they are so hospitable. If you go out in the grasslands and you pass by the tent of a family, even if they have a little bit of cheese, they will share it with you. This great spirit of giving here is what I really appreciate."

"So it is the spirit of giving of Tibetan people which keeps you here in Shangri-la?"

"Partly that, partly the way people live. The religion in daily life, and the region, all over the area are spectacular beautiful areas. If you look out at the mountains in the back, you will see the blue poppy, which is a famous flower explorers were looking for years." She pointed to a mountain behind the hotel, covered in blue flowers. Strings of *jingfan* were strung across rocks, indicating a point of spiritual power between the two peaks, a passage of energy flowing between the face of two rock surfaces.

"When I first came here, I was so charmed by the people and the region. So if Zhongdian town is called Shangri-la I think it is true because it is the gateway to Shangri-la. Beyond here you travel north towards central and eastern Tibet. They could all be called Shangri-la because they are special both in terms of scenic beauty and architecture."

"Can Shangri-la be protected? Can eco-tourism really play the role you envision and set a pattern for sustainable development?"

"I believe it takes a lot of work. Small organizations such as ours have to be aware and through practice set an example through which there is a ripple effect. We try to educate all people who come in contact with us. When we are doing treks, we go on foot, on journeys passing through so many villages and communities. We will stay with them, work with them. Slowly there is a way to influence them. Certainly in garbage management, we are showing them, teaching values as well and how to protect what they have. But for more practical and quick results it is important that institutions involved in tourism, hotels, travel companies, tour operators, guides, to be educated about what is good tourism. That is the only way to keep the culture and environment here safe. Here the tourism department is very open-minded. Our governors are amazing. We talked about the problem of garbage, of plastic bags in the valley. As of April, there will be a fine for anybody caught carrying a plastic bag. There are also major efforts being made to take down the tiles, chipping tiles off the buildings, giving buildings a facelift, re-decorating them in a style with Tibet character."

I was really amazed to hear this. Virtually every small city and town in China was virtually the same, faceless buildings with no character, covered with bathroom tiles and blue glass. Local officials think this gives a city a modern look because bathroom tiles are easy to clean. The problem is nobody bothers to clean them. But here in Shangri-la County the government was actually going against the national trend, chipping away bathroom tiles on buildings and giving them a Tibetan architecture facelift. For China, a real revolution in city planning and aesthetics was finally in the works. "That is happening right now, led by the governor," Uttara emphasized. "It is amazing. This is one of those things you want to do in eco-tourism, to protect architecture and the uniqueness of each area."

"So eco-tourism encompasses not just nature but culture, not just the protection of environment as a natural environment but the uniqueness of architectural heritage, the traditions and uniqueness of a region? Is my understanding correct?"

"Yes. But this is only part. We have to find ways of protecting the bio-diversity, leaving it as natural and as wild as possible. We have a natural reserve with a whole range of mountains at the base of

156

which we have local ethnic villages. The entire mountains are treasure of wild flowers and plants. There are some very tiny plants which are gradually going and disappearing from the other parts of the earth."

"How does eco-tourism fit in, how can it save these regions?"

"There is an effort to help two of the villages earn from tourism and protect the area. They have to protect the area because it is their own land as it is and there is also their secret mountain and their secret lake where they go to pray. So there is an eco-tourism project to help the communities earn so as to bring in as much income as possible for the local communities to allow them to preserve and sustain both their environment and life style. They in turn will conserve their own land. But we fear big developers coming in. They are now talking about one developer taking over 50 square kilometers to set up an entertainment park. That is exactly what should not happen here. That will change Shangri-la."

"An entertainment park," I was aghast at the idea. "Why do they need an entertainment park in Shangri-la? They have this kind of crass developments everywhere in China. Can't they leave Shangri-la alone?"

"Very much so," Uttara shook her head in frustration. "That is a trend all over China. Big developers go into a newly opened area. It is happening in Lijiang. It is happening in other areas of Yunnan. It is happening in other cultural heritage areas of China as well. They come in and their concept of tourism may be having an entertainment park. There are hundreds of entertainment parks all over China, I do not see why one needs to repeat it and have one here. The important thing is what is unique here. As important as what is unique of Lijiang, or unique in Dali. Each one has its own uniqueness. Here our uniqueness is that we are in a region which is one of only two hundred high bio-diversity zones in the world."

"The developers and government cannot get this point into their heads?" The reality was simple. Developers obtain planning approval allowing for the destruction of environment and culture. The village people are presented with an offer they cannot refuse. So they sell out. They often do not realize what they have and therefore are unwilling to fight for it.

"Village people are very simple," Uttara explained. "Villages every where in every community are never totally united. There are always divisions of lands, families' revenge left over from history. They can be bought. That is the danger. But through our eco-tourism work we help them to understand what they have. We do this through a story. There is a story about two frogs in a bowl of yak's cream. One frog tries to jump out but finds the cream too troublesome to handle, accepts his fate and dies. The second frog never gives up. He jumps and tries to get out. Through his jumping the cream churns into yak butter. And he is free of the cream and he can jump out. So I think that is the moral for survival of eco-tourism here. All of us who believe in sustainable eco-tourism must try to keep fighting. You must keep trying."

Surrounding her hotel are two protector mountains of the valley. It is believed that luck flows into the shoulder between the two mountains. "Yes, we rebuilt the stupa that was built by our local partner's great grandfather," she explained. "Rebuilding the pagoda was the first thing she did, before building the hotel. "And every year the staff of our hotel, print prayer flags and they are hung between the two mountains over the shoulder. The energy flows between the two shoulders." She pointed to the energy.

# Flowers in the Rain

"Om Moni Bemi Hong" is a Tibetan mantra, asking for peace on the road from which we have come, asking for peace on the road which we will travel, but have not yet traveled, but dream of traveling, one day. The words are carved in Tibetan language upon soft black stones collected from a river in Shangri-la. They are selected from the river by Tibetans passing through this place. They find the stones when they cross the river. They cross the river in search of a place. Nobody seems to know where this place is. You can only find it by crossing the river.

Sacred words, Om Moni Bemi Hong, are carved carefully on the stones, which come in different shapes and sizes, as they are picked from the river. After carving sacred words carefully, the stones are laid upon other stones placed by others who have come this way before. Eventually the stones become altars, called *manidui*. They cross the river in search of a place where there are many *manidui*.

There is a valley of legend where there are many *manidui*, one followed by another and another and another, stretching as far as the imagination can unravel, into forests where nobody goes, encircling a hill covered with *jingfan* prayer flags, which in itself is a great *manidui*. If you ask Tibetans in Shangri-la where such a place is located, they either pretend not to know, or inform quietly, that you cannot find it. If you ask others, they will think that you have lost your mind. So in searching for the *manidui*, you will save time, by not asking any questions at all.

159

If you travel through a forgotten valley which nobody really knows and the Tibetans will not speak of, you will find horses grazing on wild flowers in the sun. There are rivers which cut through the grasslands, thin rivers, maybe creeks, which twist and turn like knots of a rope and continue from where they have left, leading to where you want to go, but not telling you how to get there. You can watch them and listen to the sound of water passing through your mind. Light reflected upon patterns of water left by rain in fields overgrown with grass and flowers will give you a light feeling and for a moment you will not be able to walk any further. You may become dizzy. This is neither caused by altitude or excessive sunlight. It is a process of decomposition of your thoughts. They are disintegrating before you.

Pass through a village. The Tibetans there do not want to be bothered with such questions as directions. They have seen people come and go before. They may ignore you for some time. After persistence, they may listen to your questions, and nod. But they will not tell you what you want to hear. If you leave the village disillusioned, you may stop, sit and watch horses graze on wild flowers. At this point you will begin to lose connection with rationality which always tells you not to go further. You should now go further.

Begin to look for the place where the stones have been placed. This will appear at a place where split bamboo are fit together as an open conduct, leading water from a clear mountain stream to a point where water drips from the edge of split bamboo into a small clear pond. Many have drunk water from this water dripping place, and cleansed their hands in an act of purifying the mind. Such places indicate sacred ground. Now start to look for stones carefully. They have been placed in random locations.

This is the place of many *manidui*. They begin here, formed of soft black stones from the river with the mantra Om Moni Bemi Hong carved upon them, piled carefully to form *manidui*. Each *manidui* is made from these carved mantra stones. There is an entire row of *manidui*, one after another as far as one can see running through the forests along a trail which nobody follows,

covered with giant mushroom because nobody has tread here for a long time. The trail of endless *manidui* runs to a hill decorated with *jingfan* by people who have come and left, a sacred hill, forgotten by most, remembered by few, where *jingfan* blow in the breeze, sending their prayers to all but those who remembered to hang them upon this hill. I stumbled upon this hill, entirely by

accident, after passing by many *manidui*. Nobody told me it was there. But I had heard that there was such a place, waiting to be found because it had been left by others who did not stay long enough to remember its exact whereabouts.

Around the year 1660, Da Bao Fang, the highest ranking Lama of the White Sect of Buddhism rode on the back of a spirit ram and founded the Da Bao Temple here. In that year some 20 000 Tibetans came to lay *jingfan* on the *manidui*. This is an abandoned place. However, Tibetans often return to tie *jingfan* on the shrine hidden atop a mountain of stone, a great *manidui* surrounded by hundreds of *manidui*, hidden in forest, behind streams and some pasture. It is not always clear when and how, the Tibetans will arrive. They all arrive together to tie *jingfan* on the *manidui*. Together, they leave.

Today the place is surrounded by sacred goats, maybe descended from the sacred ram, upon who the highest ranking Lama of the White Sect rode, maybe not. They have twisted horns which grow in abstract shapes unlike normal rams. Some wear tassels like jewelry in their ears and tied to their mane. The rams have eyes which speak to you very clearly and you can understand their thoughts just by looking at their eyes. So when arriving at Da Bao Temple you should spend time talking with the rams by looking at their eyes.

I climbed the great stupa, a great *manidui*, a small sacred mountain

of prayer stones. At each step of the way there was a Tibetan prayer wheel. I stopped before each one to turn it clockwise. A Tibetan prayer wheel cannot be turned any other way. A clock can not be reversed.

Upon reaching this place covered by flickering shadows of thousands of *jingfan* prayer flags carrying wind, I suddenly remembered my life as a little boy, running outdoors, discovering my shadow. This is such a simple discovery, a shadow. But I chased the shadow and it ran away. When I ran from the shadow, it followed. When I turned away from it, it was not there. The shadow was a mystery. I ran in circles chasing it, only to find that when crossing the sun in the opposite direction, it was chasing me. How could such a thing happen I wondered, but could not, understand.

Maybe we are all chasing our shadows without knowing it throughout a lifetime but not facing the fact because our shadow is always following us when we are least aware, disappearing when we look for it, sleeping when the sun sets and awaking when the sun rises. Maybe we have not been able to understand the nature of our own shadow this entire time, during an entire lifetime. Then when we die does our shadow die as well?

I suddenly became aware of this question when sitting in the shadows of thousands of *jingfan* fluttering in the breeze. They were left behind by others whose shadows had come to this place but passed. They had forgotten to remain but had remembered to leave a *jingfan* as a prayer to spread its message on wind which might carry the prayer away when lightly touching *jingfan* mixing prayer with shadows of others who had passed, when nobody remembered to come here anymore. The tying of *jingfan* requires intention.

I thought about this when my own shadow of silence was interrupted by the screaming of a chicken. Chickens crying in the wind which touched prayer flags were neither prayer nor cry. The chickens were everywhere. They scratched dirt walking around in circles. The stone steps leading to an altar covered in prayer flags rising, and rising and rising and rising in deference to the sacredness of this place, touching clouds in the sky were actually littered with

165

chickens walking in circles screaming. I could not write this because the chickens were making too much noise. Then it began to rain. The chickens got wet and so did I. So I decided to leave and look for the temple near this great *manidui* which might give me some refuge from the rain and screeching of wet chickens.

The monks were sympathetic. They do not like chickens either. Especially when wet because they scream in the rain and in such circumstances the monks can neither sleep, or meditate. So they closed the crumbling wooden doors upon the chickens and let me sit with the goats in the rain. These were sacred goats. So I sat for a while on the wooden steps, just out of the rain, talking to the sacred goats. They stared back at me and said nothing. I knew they were sacred because I could look into their eyes and talk to them even when the monks were too busy meditating to talk to me. They were eyes which had seen many *jingfan* in a kaleidoscope of colors which left the impression that life was passing by like wind in the rain. Maybe they were waiting for the *jingfan* to dry in the wind after rain. I stared at the eyes of a goat and asked why it was raining so hard. He stared back and said nothing. I decided it was time to sit in the rain.

The monks were disturbed by this idea and asked me to stop sitting in the rain but to listen to it pouring from the rooftop of the temple, across the thin piece of bamboo, precariously balanced, which served as drainage pipe, pouring onto a black stone in the center of the courtyard outside the temple where the goats sat watching my every movement with fascination. They were fascinated probably because I was the first person who was able to stop the monks from meditating. Now we all sat around the wooden steps of the courtyard of this broken down wooden temple, me, monks and goats, watching the rain together. It poured.

It rains. Water pours. Drops from rain pour. It is the sound of water striking a bucket. Water falls and strikes in a bucket. The sound of water in a bucket is the sound of water in a bucket. That is until the bucket is removed. Then water falls upon stone under the bucket which has been removed. Water on stone makes stone become smooth due to the effect of stone in water and water on

166

stone. Black stone, cold water, cold stone, black water, cold black stone and water, water turns the stone black cold, and cold black water turns the stone, because black cold water stone becomes what it is from cold black rain dripping on stone and the rain drips cold water on stone which becomes black stone from cold black water.

The water poured off of the bamboo make-shift drain pipe which let water pour on black stone in the courtyard of this run down wooden temple. I remembered hearing as a kid that Kung Fu monks trained to be masters by sitting under dripping water and meditating. Then I decided to do this by sitting on the black stone with rain dripping off the bamboo drainage pipe on top of my head instead of the black stone. The monks tried to stop me fearing I would get pneumonia in the coolness of late Yunnan mountain summer. The sacred goats watched with fascination. They said nothing, at all.

I ended up back at Uttara's eco-tourism lodge in a warm room by a fireplace, sitting on Tibetan carpets drinking yak butter tea. The monks had sent me back after I got soaked in the rain, fearing I would get pneumonia. It felt warm after an afternoon of sitting in the rain with monks and goats trying to think about meditating with water dripping on my head in the mountain coolness of a late Yunnan summer. Clouds had passed. With them, rain. It was midnight. Guests had gone to bed. The lodge was silent. The

flowers on grasslands, spreading from the front door of this lodge into the valley wrapped in night, were asleep.

I sat there with my yak butter tea and drank it. I was thinking about sleeping flowers after rain. The cup was very warm, still half full. I stared at my shadow reflected against a candle flame, flickering lightly upon the flat surface of yak butter tea held in stillness. I was searching for Shangri-la. But I was only staring, at my shadow. This time I remembered, when searching for Shangri-la in a cup of tea, to search carefully. For the first time, I was searching without searching.

# AFTER SHANGRI-LA

*In 1933 when James Hilton wrote the classic "Lost Horizon" he probably never expected to leave generations asking the question where is "Shangri-la"? Or that his book would ignite a tourism dispute in western China over which region could call itself Shangri-la for tourist dollars; simultaneously sparking an alternative scene for China's art and culture circles searching for creative space. But believe it or not, that's exactly what happened.*

*It's amazing how a cup of café latte, or yak butter tea, can spark new ideas. A coffee chat with Ai Jing became a multi-media project documenting through film, music and writing, what could best be described as China's alternative philosophy movement in western China. Music composer San Bao and alternative film director Yang Tao joined me, together creating China's first cross-media production of "Searching for Shangri-la".*

*Our journey through some of the most environmentally sound regions left in the world, Tibet, Qinghai, Yunnan, interviewing artists, dancers, musicians, pop singers, fashion designers, writers, rock bands, environmental activists, monks running grassroots aid projects, several living Buddha, nomads, and ethnic minorities determined to hold on to their traditions. These individuals would change the way I think about China, and about the notion of Shangri-la. I learned from these free creative seekers, inspired by this region, or*

*This book is dedicated to the Nomads... in us all* _____

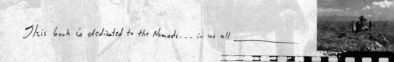

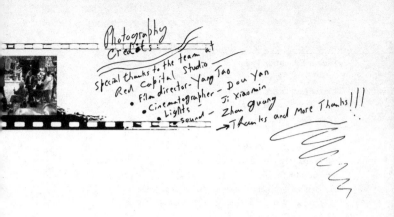

Photography Credits:

Special thanks to the team at
Red Capital Studio
• Film director - Yang Tao
• Cinematographer - Dou Yan
• Lights - Ji Xiaomin
• Sound - Zhou Guang
→ Thanks and More Thanks!!!

working to save it, that Shangri-la to them is not just a place, but a vision.

The Searching for Shangri-la project, now in its second year, seeks to capture through writing, music, photography and film the spirit of this region which has inspired a new generation of China's artistic talent.

In answer to Hilton's riddle, Shangri-la as a place can be found in China anywhere in the Qinghai-Tibetan plateau or regions exuding with values of this culture, regions sacred to the ethnic minorities inhabiting them, whose life style protects still uncontaminated parts of our eco-system. The tragedy is Shangri-la may be lost very soon due to overdevelopment, careless tourism, and short-sightedness.

In "Searching for Shangri-la" we sought to document the "lost horizon" before it is lost.

- Laurence J. Brahm
Zhongdian, Yunnan, 2003

Shangri-la · 2003

**Higher Education Press**

Publisher: *Liu Zhipeng*

General Coordinator: *Zhang Zengshun*

Acquisition: *Xiao Na, Lin Mei*

Production: *Wu Qin*

Marketing: *Hu Tao*

Responsible Editor: *Gao Ting*

Art Designer: *Wang Lingbo, Zhang Nan*

**Red Capital Studio**

Administrative Coordination: *Phoebe Wong, Song Yimeng*

Photography: *Yang Tao, Dou Yan, Zhou Guang, Ji Xiaoming*

Editorial Proofreading: *Blue Moon*

**Searching for Shangri-la**

**图书在版编目（CIP）数据**

寻找香格里拉：现代经文游记 =Searching for Shangri-la: An Alternative Philosophy Travelogue/（美）龙安志（Brahm, L. J.）著 . --北京：高等教育出版社，2004.1

ISBN 7-04-014160-4

Ⅰ.寻 ... Ⅱ.龙 ... Ⅲ.①西北地区 - 概况 - 英文 ②西南地区 - 概况 - 英文 Ⅳ
.K92

中国版本图书馆 CIP 数据核字（2003）第 126403 号

Published by Higher Education Press
4 Dewai Dajie, Beijing 100011, P. R. China
Tel: 0086-10-58581862
Fax: 0086-10-82085552
Email: limin@hep.com.cn
http://www.hep.com.cn

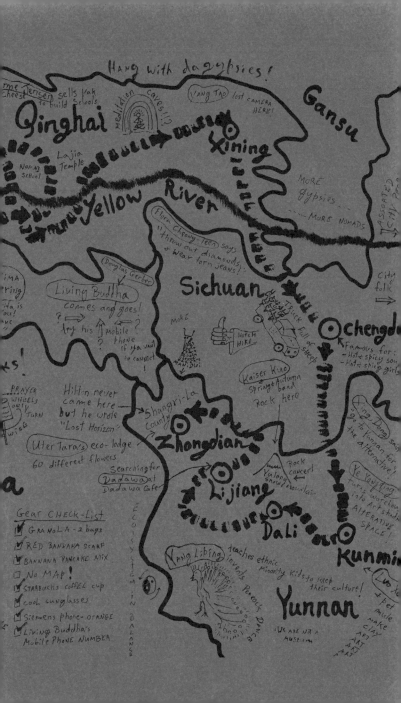